UNDERSTANDING
JILL MCCORKLE

Understanding Contemporary American Literature
Matthew J. Bruccoli, Series Editor

Volumes on

Edward Albee • Nicholson Baker • John Barth • Donald Barthelme
The Beats • The Black Mountain Poets • Robert Bly
Raymond Carver • Chicano Literature
Contemporary American Drama
Contemporary American Horror Fiction
Contemporary American Literary Theory
Contemporary American Science Fiction • James Dickey
E. L. Doctorow • John Gardner • George Garrett • John Hawkes
Joseph Heller • Lillian Hellman • John Irving • Randall Jarrell
William Kennedy • Jack Kerouac • Ursula K. Le Guin
Denise Levertov • Bernard Malamud • Jill McCorkle
Carson McCullers • W. S. Merwin • Arthur Miller
Toni Morrison's Fiction • Vladimir Nabokov • Gloria Naylor
Joyce Carol Oates • Tim O'Brien • Flannery O'Connor
Cynthia Ozick • Walker Percy • Katherine Anne Porter
Reynolds Price • Thomas Pynchon • Alain Robbe-Grillet
Theodore Roethke • Philip Roth • Hubert Selby, Jr.
Mary Lee Settle • Isaac Bashevis Singer • Jane Smiley
Gary Snyder • William Stafford • Anne Tyler • Kurt Vonnegut
James Welch • Eudora Welty • Tennessee Williams • August Wilson

UNDERSTANDING
JILL
MCCORKLE

Barbara Bennett

University of South Carolina Press

Published in Columbia, South Carolina, by the
University of South Carolina Press

Manufactured in the United States of America

04   03   02   01   00   5   4   3   2   1

Library of Congress Cataloging-in-Publication Data

Bennett, Barbara, 1959–
   Understanding Jill McCorkle / Barbara Bennett.
     p. cm. — (Understanding contemporary American literature)
   Includes bibliographical references and index.
     ISBN 1-57003-350-1 (alk. paper)
     1. McCorkle, Jill, 1958—Criticism and interpretation. 2. Women
and literature—United States—History—20th century. 3. Southern
States—In literature. 4. North Carolina—In literature. I. Title.
II. Series.
PS3563.C3444 Z59 2000
813'.54—dc21   00-008953

For my parents, ElDean Bennett and Maralin Payne Bennett

CONTENTS

EDITOR'S PREFACE

The volumes of *Understanding Contemporary American Literature* have been planned as guides or companions for students as well as good nonacademic readers. The editor and publisher perceive a need for these volumes because much of the influential contemporary literature makes special demands. Uninitiated readers encounter difficulty in approaching works that depart from the traditional forms and techniques of prose and poetry. Literature relies on conventions, but the conventions keep evolving; new writers form their own conventions—which in time may become familiar. Put simply, UCAL provides instruction in how to read certain contemporary writers—identifying and explicating their material, themes, use of language, point of view, structures, symbolism, and responses to experience.

The word *understanding* in the titles was deliberately chosen. Many willing readers lack an adequate understanding of how contemporary literature works; that is, what the author is attempting to express and the means by which it is conveyed. Although the criticism and analysis in the series have been aimed at a level of general accessibility, these introductory volumes are meant to be applied in conjunction with the works they cover. They do not provide a substitute for the works and authors they introduce, but rather prepare the reader for more profitable literary experiences.

M. J. B.

ACKNOWLEDGMENTS

I would like to thank Jill McCorkle for answering innumerable questions in person and on the phone about her life and career. When I started this project, I considered her an interesting and insightful writer; now I know she is also a wonderful human being.

I am indebted to Carolina Bennett and Michele Ritz for helping me maintain my sanity during the writing of this manuscript and to Nancy Houston and Joanne Boland Greifer for long-distance support. And to Lily for reminding me that life is more than work.

I would like to express appreciation to Carolyn Cooke, who once inspired me to become a teacher and now inspires me daily to become a better person.

Special thanks goes to my brother, Randall, my hero.

And finally to Fred Hobson, I am grateful for feedback, encouragement, time, and love.

UNDERSTANDING
JILL MCCORKLE

CHAPTER ONE

Introduction

Although Jill McCorkle has published five novels, two collections of short stories, and numerous stories and essays in journals and magazines, there has been very little critical study of her work. Perhaps this is because McCorkle has accomplished all this writing since 1984. The quantity and quality of her work is both surprising and fascinating because her career had an exceptional debut: her first and second novels were published simultaneously by the newly formed Algonquin Books of Chapel Hill. Publishing two books at the same time jump-started her career—with the "literary equivalent of a rebel yell"—and she has never slowed down.[1]

Jill Collins McCorkle was born on July 7, 1958, in Lumberton, North Carolina, a small town of just over ten thousand people in the southeastern corner of the state. Both sides of her family were long-time residents of the town, and both sets of grandparents lived within the town limits. Her father, John Wesley McCorkle Jr., was a postal worker, and her mother, Melba Collins McCorkle, worked as a medical secretary for a local pediatrician. Her parents grew up together, started dating at age sixteen, and married in August 1951. Their first daughter, Jan, arrived in 1954, and Jill was born three and half years later. McCorkle was very close to her father, who died in 1993. She claims that in many ways she was the "surrogate son" because she was the one who went fishing with her father and was told by others all her childhood that she was just like her dad. About her father McCorkle says, "I always thought he should have been the writer. He was the one who used to say, 'Wouldn't this make a fabulous story?' We'd be sitting there fishing, and he'd come up with ideas for plots."[2]

Her father, however, was not the only storyteller in her life or family. She grew up surrounded by conversation and a strong sense of the past of Lumberton. She considers her maternal grandmother, to whom she was very close, a true storyteller, and she spent many days sitting on her front porch listening to her tell family stories. Memories of afternoons at her grandmother's house were "perfect for breeding fantasy" for the young writer, she recalls: "I remember following my grandmother up and down the rows of her garden. I remember the smells of the earth and of the tomatoes, the sound of distant trucks hauling tobacco to market. The sun was warm and soothing and my grandmother's house waited at the end of the row like a cool haven. I was completely at ease in her world; I felt so secure there that it was easy to indulge in larger-than-life fantasies, to enter those bold and cocky places in my head where the aspirations were limitless."[3]

Soon she became a storyteller herself. She wrote her first story, called "The Night Santa Failed to Come," when she was seven, and she sold it to her mother for a quarter. She recalls how that changed her childhood and eventually her life:

From then on, writing was a favorite activity, particularly if I could peddle the finished product to my parents. My profit lasted only as long as it took me to mount my bicy-

cle and ride to what we called 'the little store' and then
disappeared in a little brown paper sack of Mary Janes
and Bazooka gum.

The summer after second grade my father brought
home a huge wooden crate; it had originally housed a
knitting machine delivered to a local textile mill. It was
supposed to be a storage shed, but he had no sooner cut
and hinged a door before I moved in: pallet, tea set,
dress-up clothes, my own fishing gear (another favorite
activity), bricks for a faux fireplace, and bedding for my
cat. He gave in. His tools remained crammed in a small
storage room. My mother sewed curtains for the *new*
playhouse. This became my writing place, and over the
next four years much of my time was spent there.[4]

Young McCorkle always kept a diary because she loved to
write, and she was also an avid reader. Two books that she read
over and over—and whose influence is keenly felt in several of
her own novels—are *The Diary of Anne Frank* and *The Story
of Helen Keller.* McCorkle latched onto the moving accounts of
these girls' lives and read and reread them. Because of their
strength and their independence and despite their extreme and
unusual circumstances, she could relate to what they went
through as young girls and was intrigued with their stories.

McCorkle attended Lumberton High School in the mid
1970s, and she spent most of her time, as most adolescents do,
trying to fit in with the crowd. Her essay written for *Algonquin*
called "What to Wear on the First Day at Lumberton High" char-

acterizes her adolescence as one of normal insecurities, emotional intensity, and identity exploration. She was intelligent
and popular, a cheerleader, honor roll student, and homecoming queen. What seemed like normal teenage years, however,
would become for McCorkle a ripe field of memory that she
would harvest as the setting and plot of many of her works:

> When I begin constructing a scene, though I have now
> lived in several different places, the setting that always
> comes first to my mind is my hometown—more specifi-
> cally, my hometown as it was when I was an adolescent.
> I rely heavily on that flat, pine-wooded landscape, the
> rise and fall of the traffic sounds on I-95, the way the
> light fell on my bedroom walls on a winter afternoon. I
> rely on the smells: the cool moldiness of the cemetery
> where a friend and I rode our bikes and mourned the
> deaths of people who died before we were born; the smell
> of my grandmother's kerosene heater, sitting there in the
> corner of her breakfast room; the musty halls of Joe P.
> Moore School, with its cracked plaster, ancient graffiti
> and large, rattling windows. And yes, I rely on what I
> was wearing then, and what songs were playing on the
> radio; these are the things that maintain the momentum.[5]

In 1976 McCorkle graduated from high school and left for college at the University of North Carolina at Chapel Hill—where
she found herself floundering. After living in a small town
where everyone knew her and her family, she felt out of place
and somewhat invisible in huge undergraduate classes. Then,

as a sophomore, she took a creative writing class taught by short story writer Max Steele, and things began to change. No longer was she an anonymous presence in a huge class; creative writing courses averaged under twenty people and her professors called her by name. Along with Steele, two other professors at UNC played integral roles in McCorkle's development as and desire to be a writer. Lee Smith had just started teaching at UNC, and McCorkle was in her very first class. Smith recognized McCorkle's talent immediately and praised her "wonderful sense of language" and her "unerring instinct toward speech and the inner life."[6]

McCorkle was also taught by Louis D. Rubin Jr., perhaps the most highly respected scholar of southern literature at that time. While in Rubin's class, McCorkle wrote a short story that eventually became part of her first novel. When McCorkle showed it to Rubin, he told her it felt like part of something bigger, and he was right. Eventually it became a section of *The Cheer Leader*. During her senior year, McCorkle won UNC's Jessie Rehder Prize, and her professors encouraged her to apply for graduate school. And so, after graduating in 1980 with honors (because she wrote a creative thesis—not because her GPA was high, she admits), she entered the MA program at Hollins—Lee Smith's alma mater and the college where Louis Rubin had taught from 1957 to 1967.

McCorkle's year at Hollins was an important one in her development as a writer. She took classes from well-known writers and scholars George Garrett and Richard Dillard, and she earned the Andrew James Purdy Prize for her fiction. Her thesis was a young adult novel that she doubts will ever be published.

The "voice" of the novel, however, is the early voice found in the first section of *The Cheer Leader.* After writing the young adult novel, it seemed a natural progression to expand it into what she calls the "past shots" in *The Cheer Leader*—descriptions by the protagonist of photographs from her early life.

After graduating—and marrying Steven Alexander, a young man from Lumberton—McCorkle moved to Florida, where she continued writing while teaching junior high school in Brevard County from 1982 to 1983 and working at the Florida Institute of Technology as an acquisitions librarian from 1983 to 1984. When she sent *The Cheer Leader* to Lee Smith to read, Smith referred McCorkle to her own agent, Liz Darhansoff, who sent the manuscript out to publishing houses. The manuscript was turned down several times as it kept "falling between the cracks of Young Adult fiction."[7] Needing a critique she could trust, McCorkle sent the manuscript to her mentor Louis Rubin, who—unbeknown to her—was working to establish a small publishing house which was then called Bright Leaf Books. He told her he wanted to publish *The Cheer Leader* under the new imprint, which eventually became Algonquin Books of Chapel Hill. Algonquin was developed with the idea of discovering and publishing promising new fiction writers, and McCorkle seemed perfect for the premier.

McCorkle continued writing while she was waiting for *The Cheer Leader* to be published, and in the summer of 1983, she wrote an entire novel, *July 7th.* She sent it to Rubin, who thought it was technically superior to *The Cheer Leader,* but he did not want to renege on his commitment to McCorkle's first novel. So he and coeditor Shannon Ravenel came up with the idea to publish both novels simultaneously. McCorkle certainly received more critical attention because of the dual release—as well as because of the interest in Rubin's new venture. It also helped with reviewers, who immediately had the second novel to compare to her first.

About this time, McCorkle's marriage ended, and so she left Florida and went back to Chapel Hill. Because of the favorable reviews of her first two novels, Max Steele told her he could get her a teaching slot if she were willing to be patient. Meanwhile, she worked as a secretary at the medical school—where she met her future husband, Daniel Shapiro. A teaching position materialized at UNC—and at nearby Duke as well—and McCorkle taught creative writing at both universities for a year. Shapiro graduated from medical school and accepted a residency at Massachusetts General Hospital. They married in May and moved to Boston, where McCorkle taught at Tufts University from 1987 to 1989.

While in Boston, McCorkle finished writing her third novel, *Tending to Virginia,* which was published in 1987. Two years later, a few months after the birth of her daughter Claudia, the family moved back to Chapel Hill, and McCorkle again taught at UNC while continuing to work on a new novel. In 1990 Algonquin published *Ferris Beach,* a coming-of-age novel about a young girl in a small North Carolina town. Her son, Robert, was born in December of 1991, and in 1992 the family returned to Boston, where they still live today. McCorkle's first collection of short stories, *Crash Diet,* came out in 1992 and was highly praised, winning the 1993 New England Booksellers Award. At this time, she held the Briggs

Copeland Lectureship at Harvard, which lasted for five years, and later she joined the faculty at Bennington College to teach fiction writing.

McCorkle has continued to produce novels and short stories at a remarkable pace, especially considering the complexity of her life as writer, teacher, wife, and mother. She admits that "it's a juggling act," and so she writes whenever she can find the time. She has remained loyal to the press that first published her work, and Algonquin published her fifth novel, *Carolina Moon,* in 1996. She followed up this novel with another book of short stories, *Final Vinyl Days,* in June of 1998. And despite her residence in Boston, she remains very close to her southern roots both emotionally and philosophically.

Jill McCorkle is part of what could be called the third generation of twentieth-century southern writers. The Southern Renaissance of the 1920s and 1930s saw such writers as William Faulkner, Thomas Wolfe, and Robert Penn Warren dominate the literary South. The second generation included such important female writers as Eudora Welty, Katherine Anne Porter, Flannery O'Connor, and Carson McCullers, as well as male writers William Styron, Peter Taylor, and Walker Percy. Since about 1970, however, a new generation of writers both male and female has begun writing, and although their works share many characteristics with traditional southern literature, there are also major differences—especially in the fiction of women writers.

Many of these earlier writers have had an important influence on McCorkle's writing. She credits Welty's "Why I Live At the P.O." and O'Connor's "A Good Man Is Hard to Find" as "especially inspirational," as well as Harper Lee's *To Kill a Mockingbird,* Truman Capote's *Other Voices, Other Rooms,* McCullers's *The Heart Is a Lonely Hunter* and *The Member of the Wedding,* and the Miranda stories of Katherine Anne Porter. What especially appeals to her in these stories is the strong sense of place—which, she acknowledges, is a place she knows well. The voices—and the humor—found in such stories as "Why I Live At the P.O." are something she has heard her whole life, the kind of storytelling on which she was raised.[8] In McCorkle's stories, she deals with many of the conflicts explored by these women writers who came before her: independence versus dependence, femininity versus strength, the nurturing of others in direct conflict with preservation of self, purity and virginity in opposition to sexual freedom and expression.

Although these literary ancestors have been influential in McCorkle's style and subject matter, she clearly fits into the contemporary era because of her characterizations, her attitude of affirmation, and her references to popular culture. The Women's Movement and the Civil Rights Movement deeply affected literature in the South during the 1960s and 1970s. There is still a strong sense of being "southern," but history for contemporary women writers such as McCorkle may go no further back than to the Civil Rights era, to the Vietnam War, or to the memories of a southern childhood. Her history is often private rather than a history shared by a collective southern consciousness. Some critics have suggested that southern writers today have lost the tragic sense, but it is perhaps more accurate to say that writers such as McCorkle see tragedy in a more personal sphere. The voices of her characters tell stories of a region no longer burdened by the past, but rather one that is grappling with the problems found in average homes within ordinary families.

McCorkle's works challenge and de-romanticize the southern family and its stereotypical members: "Often, in my writing," she says, "I like to populate with stereotypes—Aunt Jemima, white trash, social queen, militant black, nouveau riche, spinster—because I know there's a good chance that as soon as these people start walking and talking and thinking that they will step well beyond the boundaries."[9] Many of McCorkle's characters are in their pivotal young adult years because, in McCorkle's estimation, this is when "the emotions are working in their purest, simplest form." She believes that to "forget what it feels like to be adolescent is to forget how it *feels*—period."[10] Her young characters often begin their journey to adulthood with idealized perceptions of life, of truth, and of love. As they progress, they face tragedy and pain, and reminiscent of O'Connor's violent means for receiving personal knowledge, McCorkle's characters eventually—often painfully—come to understand that their misconceptions must be shed in order to grow and develop into psychologically sound adults. At the end of her stories, her protagonists are more often still in the process of growing, but they have come to new awarenesses that have changed their perceptions of themselves and others forever. Even when her protagonists are of adult age, they are often haunted by experiences of their youth. McCorkle believes that by the "ripe age of adolescence . . . our emotional baggage is already fully packed." We spend "the rest of our lives *unpacking,* sorting and choosing, what to treasure, what to alter, what to throw off the nearest cliff never to look at again."[11]

Growth during adolescence is only one of the themes explored by McCorkle. Another major area of concern in her writing is the woman's role in society. Her major characters are predominantly female; they are also generally feminist, though they do not always start out that way. *Tending to Virginia, July 7th, Crash Diet,* and *Final Vinyl Days* all deal with women finding themselves in situations that are not what they expected from life. They resist, they struggle, they fight back, and finally they realize that life holds for them the opportunity for change, for a fresh start, if they are willing to take the risk. Some do and some do not, but the significant factor is that it is a choice, not a sentence. Elinor A. Walker believes it is this second chance and individual liberation for women that distinguishes these third-generation southern women writers from their literary foremothers: "Their fiction suggests positive spaces for female characters to occupy—spaces not defined in relation to families, land, or community, but by the restoration of women characters as individuals."[12]

Another overriding theme in her works—which is tied both to adolescence and to the woman's experience—is the search for love in its true form. McCorkle observes that all her works deal with "accepting what is true. That what appears to be true is *not.*"[13] This is certainly the case in her characters' attitudes toward love. Idealization and romanticizing of love is a major mistake nearly all McCorkle protagonists make, characters who more than not come of age during the 1960s and

1970s—a key transitional period in society's perceptions of the female and the feminine. As her young women come to understand and accept the truth about real love and its variations, they begin to move past the illusions propagated by popular culture. This is very often an unpleasant awakening; as one of McCorkle's characters remarks in *Ferris Beach,* "'Nobody wants the truth. But sooner or later you learn that there are no fairy tales; there *is* no glamorous mother hidden on a faraway island, no prince on a white horse, no treasure chest full of jewels'" (334).

One of McCorkle's strengths as a writer, as Lee Smith has noted, is her keen sense of language—her accurate representation of conversations between real people. In a review of *Tending to Virginia* in *The New York Times Book Review,* Alice McDermott describes the novel as "three generations of Southern women . . . talking."[14] It is precisely this voice, this style, that marks McCorkle's stories as strongly southern. It is the voice of her childhood, of her grandmother telling her stories while sitting on the front porch. It is the oral tradition so clearly evident in her southern literary ancestors from Mark Twain to Joel Chandler Harris through Zora Neale Hurston and on to Eudora Welty. But McCorkle's voice is also distinctly female. Her stories rarely fit neatly into traditional plot lines. More often, strings of stories filled in gradually through memory and personal confession weave into a netted story that defies simple explanation or absolute truth.

McCorkle partly accomplishes this feat through point of view—which is never omniscient. Three of the novels—*July 7th, Tending to Virginia,* and *Carolina Moon*—are told through different, limited perspectives, each character's view telling a version of events that may or may not be accurate. *The Cheer Leader* and *Ferris Beach* are told by single narrators as internal monologues which are, of course, biased. In *Crash Diet* nine of the eleven short stories are told in first person, with the other two in third-person limited. *Final Vinyl Days* includes nine short stories separated into three sections of three stories each. In each section McCorkle writes two stories in first person and one in third-person limited. Her resistance to absolutes by not telling a story from an omniscient point of view is deliberate. Truth, she suggests, is what one knows, what one is told, what one comes to understand while growing older and experiencing life with all its unexpected twists. Truth changes depending on perspective, age, and experience. As a result, as Lynn Z. Bloom has noted, "there are no unmitigated villains, only varying degrees of goodness" in McCorkle's works.[15] And, one might add, there are no pure heroes, no characters that are less or more than simply human.

CHAPTER TWO

The Cheer Leader

Because *The Cheer Leader* was McCorkle's first novel, some reviewers immediately tried to find flaws in it that she "fixed" in her second but simultaneously published novel, *July 7th.*[1] And although that seems fair, considering the change in scope from the first novel to the second, from a first-person "thinly veiled autobiography" to a novel populated with a "cast of full-bodied characters," as Annie Gottlieb perceived it, one probably should not be too hasty in comparing and contrasting them because they are vastly different kinds of novels.[2]

In writing *The Cheer Leader,* McCorkle explores the dangers of stereotyping in the formation of character. Various novels have explored what happens to a child or young adult who is unhappy because she/he is ostracized, but McCorkle grapples with perhaps a less analyzed image—the popular girl—because readers tend to resist the idea of such a girl having any problems worth examining. Having been a popular girl herself, however, McCorkle is aware of the pitfalls in assuming that just because someone is successful and attractive, that person is happy and secure. Time takes care of most of the insecurities, but for the protagonist in *The Cheer Leader,* the danger lies in not getting beyond adolescence, in letting the temporary fears and pressures of the age become permanently debilitating.

The Cheer Leader depicts one such young southern girl's search for identity in a culture which has already clearly defined the role and stature of women. Jo Spencer—beautiful, intelligent, head cheerleader, May Queen, and member of the "in" crowd—has been taught to determine self-worth based on external signs; hence the book title, which objectifies her and labels her with what she does or what she represents rather than who she is or how she feels. Her struggle to maintain the facade of Most Popular Girl and to prove herself worthy of the honors she receives leads to her inevitable breakdown midway through her freshman year of college. When the worst happens, and Jo's weaknesses and insecurities surface, her friends and family are baffled and surprised, but McCorkle has prepared the reader throughout the novel, revealing through structure and point of view the unsteady pedestal Jo has constructed for herself through lies and self-delusion, through adherence to a belief system that is inadequate and debilitating to contemporary women of any region.

The first section of the novel is structured around a series of photographs, as if Jo is sitting next to the reader, turning the pages of an album and describing each one with phrases such as "This is Mama" and "Here, I am." Photographs are significant in many of McCorkle's works because of their ability to "freeze" time and capture an image that will never change. Since change is one of Jo's greatest fears, the security of knowing something "happened . . . that there was a moment when it was all real" is especially important to her (2). Later in the novel, Jo wishes she could do the same with events and people: "I wanted him to freeze, to stay right there" (73). This, of course, is impossible, and Jo is frustrated by her inability to control life, people, and constant shifting in circumstances.

On the other hand, photographs also infringe upon Jo's

vision of life as she believes it ought to be. She observes one picture and remarks, "I sit helplessly, unable to control what is about to happen, unable to control the story that goes with the picture" (5). This is one reason she organizes the photos chronologically and writes "B.J. (before Jo) in black magic marker" on photos taken before her birth and puts a "neat circle" around herself every time that she is present (2). In her search for an identity, she must discount events that exclude her and emphasize her presence when she appears. These actions also indicate the extent of Jo's dependence on external proof of her worth and existence, as in the picture of her on the day she was born— "proof," she claims, "that I clung to all of those times that Bobby told me that he was the real child and that I had been left in the trashpile by some black people who did not want me" (4).

Despite knowing that photographs can sometimes be "total misrepresentations of the given moment" (58), Jo clings to her illusions tenaciously. Her photographs depict seemingly happy childhood moments—birthdays, holidays, parties, big dates, and summer vacations—but the joy seems tenuous. More accurate depictions can be seen in the negatives, such as the one that shows "us standing there . . . our bodies, brownish blood red forms" with Jo feeling "a fear—a fear of being sought out, hurt, squashed like a spider on a sidewalk" (156). This image Jo holds of herself—an insect, worthy only to be "squashed" out of existence—is the truer picture, but one that can be seen only when she "hold[s] it up to the light" (156), an activity Jo shuns, for she is terrified of "exposure," a word McCorkle uses no less than twenty-five times in the novel, usually connoting vulnerability and naked honesty, the fear of feeling embarrassed or humiliated in front of others.

In one of the photographs taken at Girl Scout camp, McCorkle describes an "unexposed" and "very dark" scene in which Jo is afraid to leave her tent in the night and use the bathroom, remaining instead "under a sheet, an exposed ghost" (19). McCorkle repeats this phrase two other times in the novel, once when Jo lies to her mother about having sex with her boyfriend and once when she wakes up in a fraternity house after a one-night stand. These two later episodes are connected to Jo's confusion over her sexuality, the conflict between being a "good girl/virgin" and a "bad girl/whore." Howard, one of Jo's first boyfriends, tells her that she is "a virgin, a nobody," equating identity with active sexuality. Initially Jo rejects this dialectic and is "truly infuriated" by having to make the choice between the two. She wants to "be 'good' and 'nice'" but also to be "somebody" (53). But in her southern culture of the 1970s, a young woman could not be both: loss of virginity could still destroy a young woman's reputation, even though for a young man the loss of virginity would most likely add to his social status. Jo decides, instead, to become a "lying hypocrite" because then she can be "both good and bad" (53). After this, Jo's self-delusion escalates and she becomes increasingly unsure of who she is, anxious that her hypocrisy will eventually be "exposed." Finally, convinced that she "cannot escape S-E-X" and return to her former state of innocence and virginity, Jo writes a "pleasant" poem entitled "Amoebae," pleasant because amoebae are sexless; they "just slide around having sex with themselves" (172).

Closely tied to Jo's fear of exposure is her need for disguise and her desire for invisibility, motifs which can be found throughout the novel. From an early age, Jo adopts the habit of disguising herself by wearing costumes. When she is five years old, she envies the groundhog and wishes she too had a "nice dark hole where no one could see me." Already she feels "everyone was watching me and spying on me," and so she dresses up in her mother's heels, scarf, and bathrobe. When her father questions her about her clothing, she explains, "It was my disguise and it made me think wonderful poetic thoughts that I could not think at Kindergarten for fear that someone would hear me" (11). The bathrobe imagery—suggesting home and safety—surfaces several times in the novel when Jo feels especially vulnerable. She claims that her bathrobe is her "secret," and when things go wrong, she feels "like putting on [her] bathrobe, hiding" (40, 41). The ideas she thinks about when she is wearing her bathrobe are like no others: they are honest, they are creative, they are "exposed." She says she cannot "think the same without my robe" (46) because it is "comfortable and the pink scarf that I wore on my head seemed to hold all of my thoughts together" (19). She is "alone" in her bathrobe (55), but it is a good sensation of being alone—safe, secure, and comforted—and very unlike the image of cheerleader and beauty queen. When she is happiest—such as after she breaks off a destructive relationship with Red, the young man with whom she loses her virginity—she feels relieved "that the lies had stopped, that the old bathroom, bathrobe thoughts had returned" (138).

The bathrobe is only one of her disguises, most of which are not as obvious. She prides herself on her ability during high school to remain "still completely unexposed," only pretending to be like everyone else "as a disguise" (54). By the time of her breakup with Red, her disguise has become a permanent feature and a way to protect herself from the potential for pain. Soon after this, the world sees the first external indication that Jo is nearing an emotional breakdown. Jo describes her increasingly abnormal actions as she attempts to make her disguise concrete:

> I found an old purple dress that my mother had worn one Halloween and put it on. I teased my hair out, put on red lipstick, black gloves and dug up my mother's old lizard purse which I carried with me to Parker's drugstore. . . . I ordered a cherry Mountain Dew and sat there sipping even though I knew that everyone was staring at me. I decided the only way I could drink my drink without budging from that green vinyl stool was to pretend that I was the only person in town who was normal. It worked and when I walked outside and saw the way that the sun made everything look so sharp and clear, I decided I was going to be that way from then on. No acts, I was Joslyn Marie Spencer and I was no either/or. (142–43)

Jo has realized she can no longer be both people, the "either/or"—the young woman she really is and the facade she has fabricated—and in choosing one over the other, she chooses the fictional persona. Unfortunately for her, it is during this trip downtown in a costume that she runs into Red again, and he convinces her to give their relationship another try. Thus, her attempt at disguise is validated and she is rewarded with attention and what passes for love. Jo is not comfortable wearing a common disguise, however—sunglasses—because she dislikes disguises which are recognized by others as disguises, preferring a facade no one really knows is hiding the real Jo.

In addition to using disguises in *The Cheer Leader,* McCorkle introduces another motif in this book which she will use again in subsequent novels: holidays. Many of the photographs described in section 1 are taken on holidays—times when most people would think to get out the camera to document special occasions. Various pictures are taken on Jo's birthday, her brother Bobby's birthday, Easter, April Fool's Day, Columbus Day, Memorial Day, Groundhog Day, Halloween, Independence Day, and July 7th (McCorkle's own birthday). McCorkle uses holidays to illustrate another reality/illusion conflict: while expectations for holidays—family togetherness, gift-giving, celebration, and happiness—are usually high, in reality these special days rarely live up to most people's optimistic anticipations. And in McCorkle novels, as a character in her later novel, *Ferris Beach,* notes, "dramatic things always seem to happen around the holidays" (85).

Several of the photographs in *The Cheer Leader* are taken at a spot called Moon Lake. The moon is a symbol that McCorkle will use in more complex ways in later novels, but in this first novel it serves simply as a symbol of the illusions people prefer to believe: moonlight is much more romantic and forgiving than the glaring light of midday, and in the glow of that light, it is easier to imagine life as one wants it to be. Moon Lake is the place Jo goes with her three girlfriends, a place where boys can be watched and flirted with, and a place where Jo eventually meets Red Williams, the older boy who will bring her so much knowledge and so much pain. Red has a cabin at Moon Lake, and it is here that Jo loses her virginity, loses her identity, and later loses her faith in love when she finds Red with another girl. And in the midst of a revelation about Red's lack of loyalty to her, Jo finds herself chanting a childhood poem: "I see; I see. I see the moon and the moon sees me. God bless the moon and God bless me" (155). The romantic and illusive Moon Lake has proved instead to be a place of crushing awakening for Jo.

In *The Cheer Leader* holidays are tied to another motif McCorkle employs: allusions to historical figures. Columbus Day is mentioned more than any other day: four of the photographs described are taken on this relatively obscure holiday, and Christopher Columbus is mentioned six other times in the novel. Jo describes Columbus Day as "a very famous holiday," "a very important day," a "very sacred day," and she judges Columbus to be "the most wonderful person to ever live" (9, 15, 24, 26). Although Jo's accolades seem overstated, the significance of Columbus to Jo is tied to her ongoing search for truth. In a passage labeled October 12, 1966—when Jo is nine years old—she explains why she admires Columbus so ardently: "Right out of the blue, I will think, 'Columbus had balls' because he took a chance, because he did not base his beliefs on what other people thought, because he discovered the truth. I admire that because chances are hard to take, the truth is often difficult to face, because somewhere in the back of his mind, there must have been a slight doubt, a slight fear of finding himself clinging to the edge of the world, dropping into that pit of darkness that everyone else 'knew' was there. And yet, he kept going after the bit of proof that was necessary for his beliefs" (16–17).

As a child Jo admires Columbus for tenaciously adhering to his search for the truth, but as she grows older and is exposed to the gray areas in everyday life, she admits that sometimes "people just don't want to discover or accept a change in history, because it is easier to believe what everyone else believes" (15). Her proof of this sad truth includes the various stories told about another historical figure, George Washington. The legendary story she is told about Washington cutting down a cherry tree and then lying about it is most likely a lie— a fact made more ironic since the story is designed to teach children the importance of honesty. Then Jo hears another story about Washington, one more likely to be true: "he died of syphilis and pneumonia, the former which he got from someone other than Martha and the latter which he got on his way to see the carrier of the former" (15). Eventually, she concludes that sometimes truth is "sacrificed for ease" depending upon what is easier for people to accept: "It's all relevant," she says, "'I cannot tell a lie' is important and fucking out on Martha is not" (15). Adopting such an attitude for her own life makes living as a hypocrite much easier.

By the time the fourth October 12 photograph appears in her descriptions, Jo is eleven years old and does not even mention that the day is Columbus Day. It has become ordinary, and the search for truth hardly seems worth the effort when lying gets her so much further in life. Jo says nothing more about

THE CHEER LEADER

Columbus and his search for truth until she is sixteen and admiring the view at Moon Lake. She admits there "was a time when such a sight would have brought to mind Christopher Columbus," but "I had other things on my mind" (56). Jo no longer craves truth because lying has become so much more convenient; therefore, Columbus has become less attractive to her. At the time of her breakdown in college, Jo begins a confusing composition by debating whether or not Columbus was Jewish. The paper deteriorates into near stream-of-consciousness, and Jo finally concludes: "If Columbus was or was not Jewish really isn't important" because "he took a chance and I have recently heard that there is no room for chance in a deterministic society" (227). Not only has the truth become insignificant in comparison to the illusion she has carefully constructed for herself, but she has also decided that society no longer has a place for people who take risks in the name of truth.

By the time section 2 begins, it is clear that Jo is well on her way to an emotional disaster. The entire section is told in first-person point of view, but McCorkle changes from past to present tense several times during this part of the novel when Jo is struggling with depression and self-doubt. Each time the text shifts to present tense, it is during an encounter with Red— when Jo lives completely in the moment, ignoring the past of who she was as well as her connections to her family, friends, and culture. When the scene is over, McCorkle returns to past tense, and Jo is once more connected to her surroundings by time and space. As soon as Red appears on the scene, Jo steps out of herself and seems to observe her behavior from the outside as it is happening, as if it is another girl doing the things with Red that she would rather not admit she is doing. This happens at least four times in section 2, with the tension between her two realities becoming more acute and her identity becoming more fragmented.

Along with Red—whose name signifies danger as well as passion and sin—another character plays an important role in Jo's conflict. Beatrice, a social pariah Jo meets first in a preschool class called Tiny Tots, is, in fact, Jo's alter ego. In her dissertation, "Redefining Southern Fiction: Josephine Humphreys and Jill McCorkle," Elinor A. Walker identifies Beatrice as the "child-like, inner misfit self that Jo has been afraid to expose."[3] Beatrice is what Jo would be if she did not wear the disguise and play the role of cheerleader and all it connotes. By the time the girls enter junior high school, Jo articulates the differences between them, labeling herself "fit" as in "survival of the fittest" and labeling Beatrice a "misfit, one who is not in shape, one not fit enough to survive among the rest, as part of the rest" (54). At this point, the two girls seemingly pursue opposite paths: Jo becoming head cheerleader and May Queen and Beatrice socializing with the other "misfits" at Moon Lake, using drugs, and becoming sexually active. Below the surface, however, the girls are still very much alike.

When Jo discovers Red with another young woman, it is, of course, Jo's alter ego, Beatrice. When Jo finds Beatrice on Red's bathroom floor—drunk, sick, and helpless—she also finds herself there, and she decides she hates Beatrice and, in effect, hates the girl Jo fears is inside herself, waiting to be exposed. Beatrice tells Jo, "'You've got everything, do you know that? . . . I just wanted a little of what you have, Jo"

(153–54), words Jo will echo later to her brother Bobby, whom she has placed on a pedestal the same way Beatrice has done with Jo: "'Maybe I just wanted a little of what you've got, you know? You've got everything, Bobby, you've always had everything'" (224). Such misconceptions of others' happiness lead to personal despair, and eventually Jo learns that "Beatrice had slit her wrists and bled like a stuck pig" (158), surviving, but barely. This incident is the catalyst for the final decline in Jo's emotional state. Fearing that she is somehow responsible for Beatrice's fate and should therefore share that fate, she ponders the question: "Am I like Beatrice?" (161). In her search for an answer, Jo writes a poem "'about Beatrice. It's about not fitting in,'" in which Beatrice is a "sick, helpless creature" (247). Her therapist, however, immediately recognizes that Jo has written a poem about herself.

Many of the problems Jo faces in this tale of initiation come about because of her inability to establish her own code of behavior. Jo is part of a generation of women who came of age in the 1970s—a time when rules and roles for women were being questioned and reinvented. Having left the old expectations of femininity behind, young women like Jo needed to determine new codes and new definitions for themselves. At one point, Jo laments the lack of clear-cut rules in her life and era: "I had always wished that I had belonged to the previous generation where there were rigid rules and convictions, where certain appearances were upheld just like in cheer leading, team sports, the Olympics, National Honor Society" (78). Jo mistakenly believes that following rules will protect her from problems, and so she creates strange and restrictive rules for herself concerning food, studying, and even television watching. Her behavior is unrealistic and immature, for growth and maturity—along with sexual experience—are inevitable. But partly because of her generation, partly because of her cultural upbringing, Jo is unprepared to replace the old rules for women with meaningful and realistic new boundaries.

Despite her frantic efforts to get her life under control and because she sets such impossible high standards of stoic behavior for herself, she fails by breaking more rules. Finally she concludes, "After the rule has been broken once, it doesn't matter. Isn't that what they say about a virgin?" (191). She still cannot see past the either/or existence: either she is a perfect, asexual angel or she is a terrible, sexual whore, and during the first semester of her college year, she swings from one extreme to the other.

In her attempt to control her life, Jo has a bout with anorexia, brought on partly, it is suggested, by Red's earlier comment: "'If it's one thing I can't stand, it's a woman who doesn't take care of her body'" (186). This condition is tied to several other urges and insecurities as well. First, Jo recalls longingly her childhood, when decisions were not so difficult and behavior was clearly defined. Anorexia is her attempt to make herself "smaller," and thus more invisible. Losing body fat makes her body less female/less sexual, therefore more childlike and innocent. When her friends confront her with her weight loss, she protests, "There is simply too much of me; there is way too much" (148), and when she feels guilty about her treatment of Beatrice, she says, "I'm not fit anymore. . . . Must get thin, stay small, stay very little so that people can't see me" (161). Starving herself also expresses her need to punish herself for her sexual "sins"—that is, the sin, as she sees it, of growing up and losing her sexual innocence—as well as being a way to control at least one aspect of her life that seems out of control. Since she has broken her rules, she feels that everyone can see she is a hypocrite, but by staying small, she can evade the knowing glances of condemnation she imagines are being sent her way.

In section 3—which describes Jo's first year at college and her descent into depression and despair—McCorkle establishes Jo's objectifying of self and emotional fragmentation by writing the narrative in third-person point of view, a shift which accentuates Jo's disguise and need to distance herself from her own life. The need to follow rules increases in this section; once again Jo states that rules "must be followed to a tee or something horrible will happen" (206). The narrative is filled with Jo's statements that she "must" do this or do that, such as "She must read in the hall where it is light" (172), "every step must be the exact same stride" (213), and "She must go back to the original rules" (226)—all in an attempt to avoid adult choices.

The one situation that seems to give Jo stability and strength is her poetry class. It is the only class that she attends regularly and is, therefore, the only class in which she earns a good grade. At first she seems to like poetry because it makes her feel safe; there are "correct words" and strict rules of structure (165) as well as opportunities to feel "worthy" (169). Poetry makes "everything else bearable" (219), and she finds herself quoting poetry in times of stress. Eventually, though, Jo appreciates her ability to express herself in poetry, and she begins to discover her identity through its creation. Through poetry Jo realizes the question of identity has a simple answer; that is, she must experience life, take risk, and accept change—all on the road to creating the person Jo will become and fusing the internal and external Jos. After Jo stands up in class to read her own poem, she thinks, "It is not good, but it is not bad; it is a good time to be in the middle" (251). For the first time, Jo resists seeing her world as either/or; she is content to be neither extreme.

In the final few pages of the third section, Jo begins to make decisions and accept change in her life. She begins seeing a therapist and starts eating normally again. She notes with pride that one day is very important because "it was the first time" that she had really been honest with her therapist, trusting him so much that she "exposed herself" to him (245). Symbolically, she cuts her hair—which she had grown long because that "'is how Red always wanted it to get'" (195)—signaling her separation from both Red and her need to make other people happy at the expense of her own desires. Most important, she begins living life without rules, and McCorkle's verbs change from "must" to "can" and "could," as in "She can have friends. She can just walk around all day and eat dry cereal if she wants to. She can do anything that she wants to do" (256–57).

In the final section McCorkle shifts back to first-person point of view, a change indicating Jo's movement toward development of an identity. This section takes place several years later when Jo is twenty-three and brings together many of the earlier images and ideas utilized in the first three sections. Jo has spent several years in therapy and is slowly improving, and, generally, she has stopped lying to herself and others, instead focusing on being honest and trusting others to accept her as she is. McCorkle sets this final section at Moon Lake, but Jo claims "Red Williams is no longer a part of Moon Lake" (262). She sleeps at night without nightmares now, but admits that the "gray blend that separates night from day" still frightens her (259). It would be easy in this final section for McCorkle to present a woman who has come through therapy successfully, made whole and able to face reality with no misconceptions, but McCorkle resists presenting such a rosy ending. The grayness Jo fears is still that area between either/or—neither black nor white, but that unclear area in the middle where individual decisions about behavior must be made. And Jo is making them, slowly. She comments: "Presently, I have many choices to make. . . . *The Feminine Mystique* says that you don't have to be an either/or and I am convinced that this is true, that there is a safe inbetween" (264). She continues to look for herself somewhere between the extremes, where she will be comfortable, safe, and content.

Clearly, though, issues of truth and illusion still trouble her, and she continues to work out the complexities of both. As she imagines the future, she sees herself falling in love and having a son, and in this fantasy both Columbus and Washington surface again in her thoughts: "Then I will paint the Pinta, the Nina and the Santa Marie so that he will know historical facts. I will not yet tell him that it is believed by many scholars that Chris brought V.D. to the new world. And isn't that something? If it hadn't been for Chris, the father of our country never would have gotten syphilis! How fascinating, the things that hold humanity together, the things that hold people together" (263). Although it may appear Jo is still denying reality by imagining herself withholding truth from her son, the word "yet" indicates a recognition that some truth is best revealed at a propitious time when the listener is prepared to understand it. In addition, it is clear that Jo has learned some disturbing facts about her hero, Columbus, yet still admires him, a sign that she is able to accept imperfection in others and perhaps in herself.

She also mentions that she will show her son "old pictures" of herself in her cheerleading outfit and as Most Popular. Unlike her mother—who once showed Jo a picture of herself and a boy who was not Jo's father—Jo will not show her son a picture of herself as the May Queen because it "would upset him" to see her with a man who is not his father (265). Obviously, Jo has settled some questions about reality and illusion, but her growth is still tenuous. She has made progress, but she "still can't wear sunglasses" (263), for example. She is still unsure of herself sexually, but McCorkle's imagery suggests cautious growth, fertility, and safety in the future: "I will count the sexless single celled creatures and I will make sure that each has its very own home, its own life, and I will make the lake grow and grow, to spread and rise, slowly, cautiously, spinelessly, I will make it grow so that it will look just like it used to look, the way that I remember it all" (267).

Change is no longer as frightening to Jo as it once was, and as she pictures getting older, she imagines "exposing" herself. Her identity is incomplete, but she knows she is "a little bit of everything that I've ever been" (266). Instead of trying to return to the innocent past, she is allowing herself to move slowly ahead: "At least right now I know that I am moving, sliding, changing" (266). No longer feeling the need to hide, she ponders: "I have gotten so big that the world is getting smaller, or is it that there is something out there so big that it has no answer, definition, beginning or end that makes it all seem so small?" (266). She has realized that "exposure" of truth will not cause others to stop loving her, and so Jo is able to confront reality and realize there "is a choice to make, a chance to take" (267).

Along with exploding the myth of the popular girl, *The Cheer Leader* exposes a universal female fear of being judged solely by outward signs. Such criteria force women to focus on the facade—at the peril of losing the self. McCorkle's first novel is *The Bell Jar* for the last part of the twentieth century; Jo Spencer experiences an extension and intensification of the frustration and confusion Sylvia Plath's narrator feels as both choices and dangers multiply for women in the South and in all of America. The hope in McCorkle's novel is located in Jo's future, in the tentative progress she continues to make in developing an identity that is real, rather than one that is based on external labels such as "cheer leader" and "popular" as indicators of worth.

CHAPTER THREE

July 7th

July 7th became a novel out of sheer nervousness, as McCorkle explains it. While waiting for word on the publication of her first novel in the summer of 1983, she began writing to keep her mind occupied, working at least eight hours a day on the novel and finishing it in just a few short months. With an immediate comparison available, not only were reviewers able to see that McCorkle could write in different styles and on many different subjects, but they also were able to see her mature from one novel to the next. Annie Gottlieb reviewed both novels for *The New York Times Book Review,* describing McCorkle's evolution as "startling." She notes that McCorkle aptly moved from *The Cheer Leader*— "a good but familiar first novel showing glimmers of wicked talent"—to *July 7th*—"a book bighearted enough to embrace a whole small town," and one which marks McCorkle as "a full-grown novelist."[1]

In many ways *July 7th* is a radical departure from *The Cheer Leader.* The action of the novel is contained in twenty-four hours beginning with the murder of Charles Husky, night clerk at the Quik Pik convenience store. Instead of using a single narrator, McCorkle employs no fewer than twenty voices. By telling the same story from a variety of points of view, McCorkle emphasizes that what people believe to be truth is often only one person's version of the truth—an issue she deals with in *The Cheer Leader* and a topic she addresses in all of her subsequent novels and many of her short stories. The significance of perspective is emphasized in a short scene in which a rich man's daughter, Frances, accidentally runs over a young girl's cat. Frances imagines her role in the scene one minute as "the blonde that looks like Farrah Fawcett that was driving the Datsun 280–ZX, that ice-gray Datsun that ran over her kitten," but immediately after sees herself from a different view: "that awful streak-haired woman in a skimpy coverup driving a gray killing machine that ran her cat down and killed him."[2]

In writing the novel, McCorkle began only with the idea of two characters: Sam Swett—one of two supposed witnesses to Charles Husky's murder—and Juanita Weeks, a woman who cannot distinguish reality from fantasy and whose marriage collapses after her husband discovers her "in a prostrate position on top of some crates" with Ralph Waldo Emerson Britt (a man whose name ironically is associated with wisdom and common sense) in the meat freezer of the local Winn Dixie.

As in *The Cheer Leader,* holidays play an important role in this novel. The story is set three days after Independence Day, on Granner Weeks's eighty-third birthday. Granner has decided to combine the two holidays and so plans her own birthday party for the afternoon. The day has already begun badly, though, with the murder of Charles Husky, and events do not improve much throughout the day. A time set aside for celebration turns into a family feud during which everyone's dark secrets, fantasies, and lies are exposed—all of which Sam Swett witnesses and absorbs. In effect, the novel is Sam's initiation story—or at least the second half of his initiation—for Sam has already been disillusioned with life during his stay in New York City, from which he is returning when he becomes a witness to murder. As the story begins, Sam is riding with a trucker, and he is singing bits and pieces of songs which reveal the life he has left in the city: "*If you like action come to NYC / they got murder and rape and robbery, / they got all kinds of violence can happen to you, / they got broken glass and dog doo-doo, / a Saturday night special every night of the week*" (1). McCorkle presents a classic case of idealist meeting reality, and in response Sam has decided to become a fiction writer—to "create worlds that are worlds better than this piece of crap" (1), and he has shaved his head as a symbol of shedding his old life for a new one. Sam is a modern-day Huck Finn, naive and pure until he is faced with life's daily cruelties.

In a guileless artist-to-be style, he believes he can rise above the stench of the world, "eat just enough to keep him alive, detach himself from the gluttonous world, remain an individual even though everything else is becoming the same, then he will be able to tell it, in his own words" (65). He wants to "be the one that sums everyone else up, to be the observer, not the one that's being observed" (233). Despite his desire to be detached and unique as a writer, his efforts at both image and content are only imitative of great writers. To be a great writer, he believes he must live as they have lived, as "alcoholics, homosexuals, suicidal, schizophrenic," and write words that "only the author understands" (67, 68). It is with this naive attitude that Sam enters Marshboro, North Carolina. In a short twenty-four-hour period, however, he learns that an artist, of all people, must understand the world and participate in life in order to be able to write about it convincingly and honestly.

Although finding Charles Husky's body is Sam's most dramatic episode in Marshboro, his most significant is meeting, talking, and finding romance with Corky, a waitress at a coffee shop and great-niece of Granner Weeks. Corky and Sam "complete" each other as a whole person because they are essentially opposites, each offering the other what she/he needs. When Sam first meets Corky, he has lost faith in the world and his ability to survive in it, afraid he will be seduced into the homogeneity of living. The disillusionment Sam has experienced is part of the normal process of initiation, as Joseph Campbell has explained in his book *The Man with a Thousand Faces.* In this process, a young man must reject the status quo and the traditionally held cultural beliefs before he can discover truth, progress toward his own potential, and reconcile with the world, accepting both the positive and negative aspects of living. And Corky becomes his guide.

Initially, Sam seems to think that he will be the one who teaches Corky about the world. After all, he thinks, it is he who has been out in the world, experiencing the hardships of New York living. He warns Corky that "the world [is] violence and death" (185), and he cautions her against associating with Sandra, another waitress, because Corky "'might get to be like her. [She] may fall in the hole with everyone else'" (186). It is Corky, however, who truly knows of the difficulties life offers. She had discovered her father "'with his head blown off'" and as a result had watched her brother deteriorate mentally until he "'wound up in a hospital making doll babies out of corn'" (262, 264). Whereas Sam has faced the sadness of the world and then turned away from it to hide, Corky has survived and even thrived, stronger because of what she has experienced. She teaches Sam that what he is feeling is fear and loneliness—normal reactions that all humans feel.

Through his association and "apprenticeship" with Corky, Sam comes to some significant realizations. At one point during Granner Weeks's party, McCorkle writes, "This is the first time in his life that he's thought that maybe everybody feels a little different at some time or another" (256), revealing the depth of his naïveté before this point. He also begins to enjoy "fitting in" and "knows that he wanted to fit in, to be liked and accepted," and he credits Corky with somehow making it possible (308, 260). Finally, Corky convinces Sam to return to his family by contrasting her own dreams of belonging with Sam's desire to be isolated: "'You see I'd give anything if I could say that somebody cared so much for me that every thought in their head near about went in my direction, or if I could say that I had a home and family where I could go when I pleased and never be alone. You say that you want to be alone and all I know is that you must not have ever really been that way'" (367). The final two pages of the novel show a new Sam, having called his parents to come and take him home. His dream of being a writer is on hold while he gives himself "time to let his hair grow, to get cleaned up, to decide what he wants to do" (386). He has accepted that his life is both different and similar to others' lives and that this is what makes life interesting and worth writing about.

Sam's coming of age is only one of the stories that McCorkle has woven into this novel about dreams and reality. Various other characters are engaged in relationships and situations requiring them to separate what is real from what is not, and Granner Weeks's birthday party—a scene which encompasses over half the novel's pages—is the catalyst for both accusations and epiphanies of various kinds and degrees. Juanita Suggs Weeks and her husband Harold—son of Granner Weeks—have recently separated because of Juanita's Winn Dixie episode. Juanita's fantasy life is so real that she can no longer distinguish between true life and the life she daydreams about while stretched out on her velvet bedspread. Even when Harold discovers her with Ralph Britt, she is sure it is a dream and she will soon wake up. Returning to reality occurs slowly for Juanita, so deeply is she involved in fantasy. Forced finally to face her very corporeal adultery, Juanita sets out to win back Harold when she encounters him at Granner Weeks' party, but not before all the other guests at the celebration face truths of their own—with Harold as the unmasker and tormentor.

Tied closely to the theme of reality and illusion is McCorkle's social satire—specifically aimed at class in this novel. The line between truth and fiction is blurred by the lies characters tell themselves about the past, their families, and their social rank. McCorkle satirizes social structure by illustrating the absurdity of determining internal worth based on external indicators—that is, economic background. Ernie Stubbs and his wife Kate (sister of Harold) have spent their adult lives trying to move up the rungs of the social ladder. Perpetually embarrassed by his lower-class upbringing on Injun Street, Ernie, along with Kate, has fabricated a whole new life: wearing the right clothes, shopping at the right stores, attending the right parties, and associating with the right people. Despite his seeming success—many people are surprised to find out the truth about Ernie's roots—he continues to struggle with living a lie. Throughout the novel McCorkle associates cat imagery with Ernie to express his conflict between feeling legitimately "pedigreed" versus feeling like an alley cat who has been brought into the parlor. Ernie is also struggling with dreams of adultery, an act he associates with power and social position—but also, conversely, with lack of class. When his secretary, Janie Morris (perhaps alluding to the famous Morris the Cat from television commercials), shows interest in him, he first thinks not of the sexual act but of his cat "Booty," who did not care if her mate came from pedigreed lines. Like his suggestively named cat, Ernie wonders if his background should really matter at all, knowing instinctively that social level does not determine action or dictate goodness.

When Janie Morris continues to pursue him, though—literally "creeping closer, like a cat" (43)—he succumbs and has sex with her on his office floor late one night. His initial response is the feline mating call of "MMMrrreeeeooo-owwwww!," but later he finds himself having conflicted feelings—both "cheap, used" and "powerful and manly" (68) and experiencing "as much shame . . . as he ever did over on Injun Street" (72). He continues to battle internally over whether or not his actions mark him as sophisticated and powerful or trashy and base. The cat comparisons continue at Granner's party, when Kate tells Ernie that their granddaughter is distressed about her tomcat being run over that morning, commenting, "Serves that ugly old tomcat right for being out and prowling." Ernie feels the need to defend his feline parallel. As a human tomcat, Ernie rationalizes his own behavior by justifying the cat's: "It just doesn't seem right that a tomcat would be punished for simply doing what he was put on earth to do, even a male pedigreed would do the same" (150–51).

In spite of Ernie's nagging notion that background should not matter, Ernie and Kate continue to pursue social status, often choosing appearance over substance. After the birthday party, for example, they must choose between visiting their daughter and just-born grandchild at the hospital or arriving on time to a social engagement. That they choose to attend the party says much about their priorities and values. McCorkle leaves the reader with the distinct feeling, though, that it is Kate, not Ernie, who understands and aspires to this kind of life. Ernie has difficulty determining "value," and so he resorts to buying the most expensive items to ensure quality. He is enticed and seduced, though, by Janie's inexpensive perfume, suitably named Tigress.

Adding to the social satire, McCorkle weaves in parallel stories of other characters grappling with class issues. Kate and Ernie's daughter Rose misses the birthday party because she is at the hospital, giving birth. Rose is a product of her parents' social dreams, and the scene highlights her inability to cope with reality. Brought up to believe that rich people are naturally superior and therefore do not experience pain as poor people do, she is distraught to learn that she must endure labor like anyone else. In a concurrent scene back at the party, Juanita overhears her teenage daughter Patricia confessing to her Aunt Kate that she is ashamed of her mother and of her home. McCorkle offers no easy answer to this particular dilemma. It is a painful scene, and both Patricia and her mother elicit sympathy. The shame, McCorkle may be suggesting, comes not from wishing for a better life for oneself but in the practice of society determining a person's worth based on socioeconomic group.

Several other situations and characters support this asser-
tion. At different positions on the social scale, McCorkle presents Corky, Officer Bob Bobbin, and finally the Foster family.
Corky is a poor girl, living in a boardinghouse, working as a
waitress. Despite her background and financial situation, it is
Corky who is perhaps the most honorable and ethical character
in this novel. She discounts race when choosing friends, she offers
her time and energy to her neighbors in need, she befriends
lonely and seemingly destitute Sam Swett, and she has a clear
understanding of who she is and what she desires.

Bob Bobbin, on the other hand, proves that lack of background does not guarantee goodness any more than money
guarantees taste. McCorkle has a great deal of fun with Bob
Bobbin. As his name implies, she means him to be a comic
character, alluding to the song about the red robin who comes
"bob bobbing along." McCorkle even describes him as looking
like "a bird with that sharp nose and large Adam's apple like a
turkey" (52) and has other characters refer to him as a "bird
cop" who "perches." (He appears again in her fifth novel, *Carolina Moon,* but is much less clownish and absurd. Wanting the
reader to take Bobbin more seriously in that novel, McCorkle
calls him "Robert" instead, minimizing allusions to the song.)
In *July 7th* Bob is used to illustrate an extreme of type. He is
the closest McCorkle gets to stereotyping in this novel. He has
comically bad taste, choosing to decorate his new apartment in
"red shag and that black and red sort of velvety paper." His
taste is a cliché, running toward Elvis and Marilyn Monroe
items, "or one of those coiled up cobras," all of which he
believes is "quality art" (151). He drinks champagne called

Champale—sold in six-packs—and naively believes all this makes a favorable impression on women.

Such obvious stereotyping aside, however, there is more going on inside Bob's mind than planning his next decorating debacle. Bob, like everyone else in the novel, desperately wants to be accepted and needed—a compulsion he may be trying to satisfy with his job as a policeman. He, like Ernie Stubbs, desires to move up on the social scale, but unlike Ernie, Bob lacks the knowledge and connections he needs to do so. Paralleling Ernie's attempts to socialize with people "above him"— people who generally laugh at him behind his back—Bob's artless attempts to improve himself fall short, and instead he appears merely foolish without ever realizing it. Bob misunderstands wealth, believing it is a cure-all. Even his work as a policeman has taught him nothing; he still believes that class determines behavior and that "no child raised in a fine home in a nice neighborhood" is capable of committing a crime (267).

The Fosters, the top link on the social chain, are an old-money family in comparison to Ernie and Kate, social icons who hold a dinner party on July 7th and who seem more concerned with the success of their social affair than with their troubled family life. In the kitchen during the party, their son Billy confesses to killing Charles Husky at the Quik Pik, but instead of calling the police, the Fosters use their money and influence (as McCorkle notes they have done before) to clean up the mess their son has made and make the problem go away. Instead of going to jail, Billy is simply sent off to Montana to a dude ranch, and his accomplice, a doctor's son, is sent to Denver to school, attesting to the power of position and wealth in determining what is known to the world as truth. Dave Foster attempts to use his position further to protect his son, offering money to his housekeeper, Fannie McNair, who overhears Billy's confession, but perhaps it is Fannie's position as a black servant that keeps her from accepting the bribe; she knows that wealth alone will not change her life as a black woman, and so she prefers not "'to take that kind of money'" (371).

Fannie's role in this novel brings to light another important issue that McCorkle satirizes: race. Sam Swett again plays the role of observer and philosopher, Bob Bobbin is the struggling example, and Corky represents the moral role model. In the first scene of the novel, when Sam is riding with the trucker, McCorkle includes a stream-of-consciousness sequence that at first seems a meaningless drivel from a drunk and disturbed young man, but as the novel progresses, his words grow in significance. In the passage, Sam rants about food—Chef Boyardee, candy bars, Fritos, Ruffles, etc.—but he focuses most on his memory of eating M&Ms:

> He remembers eating M&Ms: he would sit down and open the pack, segregate before eating; there were blacks, light skin blacks, Indians, Chinese and Martians; there were no white M&Ms; there was no race with orange skin; orange ones were the white people, no other choice, but then came the big decision, which race do you devour first? And he got older but there were still M&Ms, same wrapper, only difference that the Indians had become extinct, stripped from society, made children hyperactive. He would segregate them, figure the population percentages,

integrate them back within the bag and pull them out one at a time, try to guess which race was melting in his hand before he popped it into his mouth. . . . What do kids do now? There are no colors for Puerto Ricans, Cubans, India Indians, Iranians. It would be so difficult to be a child, so difficult to segregate and discern the differences, just say they're all M&Ms, they're all people. (5)

Clearly, Sam is struggling with the concept of race, with the role white males have played in determining who merely survives, who prevails, and who becomes extinct. Instinctively, though, he knows all people, like all M&Ms, are the same below their colorful surface; in his hand, they all feel the same.

Later, at Granner Weeks's party, when Bob Bobbin and Harold use the word "nigger," Sam feels uncomfortable, knowing it isn't "right to call black people niggers, not right at all, a violation of civil rights, people are just people." He knows that, like M&Ms, people can be "homogenized" if only they can "escape from their society within the bag" (53–54). At this point, however, Sam chooses not to speak out; he is still observing and recording for future reference as a writer. As Sam progresses, though, his thoughts evolve and mature, and he is able to verbalize his observations about real people and racism. He feels bothered, for example, by a small black boy playing with a white G.I. Joe and "cannot help but wonder what it must have felt like to be a black child with a white baby doll, to be a black child and for Roy Rogers and all the good heroes to be white" (311–12).

Bob Bobbin also struggles with racism, but his is not so

obviously a winning battle. Superficially, Bob plays the easy role of racist: he uses the term "nigger" freely, he tells Corky that she "ain't got no business living someplace with niggers," and he arrests a black man—Thomas, Fannie McNair's son—as the prime suspect in Charles Husky's murder simply because Thomas cannot prove his whereabouts at the time of the murder and because he fits Harold's generic description of a black male. Thomas, perhaps Bob's black parallel, is equally stereotypical: he has a white girlfriend because it gives him status and because he knows his mother "'wouldn't like the notion of him being with a white girl,'" he plays the part of angry young man because his mother works for white people, and he believes that "nothing's gonna change" for him, simply because he is black and will therefore be forever oppressed by the white race (316, 201).

Bob's real story is more complex than it appears, though. Because McCorkle tells Bob's story through his own eyes, his confusion about race becomes clear. Earlier in his career, Bob had saved a black man's life by giving him mouth-to-mouth resuscitation, and he received for his efforts an "outstanding service plaque." While Bob feels proud of his heroic act, his fellow officers taunt him with "Kissed a nigger," and "Did you slip the tongue?" (79). In an effort to avoid the ridicule, Bob minimizes his heroism, refusing to put up the newspaper article about it on the bulletin board. Obviously, though, Bob is confused. On one hand, he "can't help but think about it, to remember how he pumped that man's chest and breathed life back into him," but on the other, society—or at least his society—sends him the message that his effort was less important because the man was black (80). He hopes that by finding the black murderer of Charles Husky, a sort of balance will be restored: perhaps he believes that by arresting and condemning one black man, it will make up for saving the life of another. Then, he hopes, "he can go back to saying Negro or black outside of the station. . . . then he could be proud of the way that he saved that old man's life" (158).

Bob Bobbins inspires less hope for change than Sam Swett does, though. While Sam is willing to consider individual change apart from society's standards, Bob can only change within the confines of the social order in which he already lives. In contrast to both of these characters, McCorkle presents Corky, who again plays the part of role model and balancer for Sam. Her friendship with Fannie McNair transcends at least two social barriers: Corky is young and Fannie is a grandmother, and Corky is white and Fannie is black. McCorkle symbolizes their friendship and strength in the boardinghouse they share: the house "is at the edge of town, separated from the bottoms only by a broken-up and overgrown railroad track. What little brick is left unexposed by the creeping vines is dark with age, and it seems at a glance that could all crumble down with the slightest tremor, yet the brick is very strong, its texture intact, only the appearance has changed" (13). Like the house, the women are separated from the rest of the town by their attitude toward race. They would appear to be society's underlings—an old black woman who cleans house for rich white people and a poor waitress who lives alone—but in fact, these two women are not weak or inferior at all: they are the real core of strength in this novel. They alone are completely moral. They are not hypocritical. They show true charity and love for others—regardless of the way they are treated in return and regardless of the social or economic station of those in need.

Unfortunately, their moral example goes unnoticed by virtually everyone—until Sam, the observer who finally learns to see, watches the two women conversing in one of the final scenes. He hears them talk casually about the differences between being black and being white, and he is amazed at their lack of self-consciousness. Pretending that someone is not black or white, McCorkle argues, is as absurd as suggesting someone is not male or female—but the test comes in the treatment of that individual.

McCorkle begins in *July 7th* what will become one of the trademarks of her fiction: the use of popular culture in the lives of ordinary people in the South as a social comment. Whereas earlier novelists such as Wolfe, Warren, and Faulkner seemed tied to the impact of history on the present, McCorkle makes it clear that today's southerner is a product less of history than of popular culture. Music—and movies in some of her other works—propagate the illusions characters believe in contrast to the reality they often deny. Throughout the novel various characters, when faced with real life, relate what is happening to them to music lyrics. In short, instead of art imitating life, individuals' lives seem real only in relation to the songs that chronicle universal events. Life becomes a cliché rather than a unique experience.

McCorkle begins the novel with Sam Swett chanting the lyrics to "Talking Big Apple —'75" by Louden Wainwright, a song which lists the violence and vice found in New York City. Sam's reaction to such a life is to escape to another, extreme in its contrasts—that is, the life of a Florida beach dweller described in the songs of Jimmy Buffett. In between northern and southern extremes, he accidentally discovers his real life and his real history, ending up just a few miles from the town where his parents live. Charles Husky also relates real life to music. When the two young men who will eventually kill him first enter the Quik Pik, he feels sorry for them based on the way they look and casts one boy as the character in a song about blue-collar living called "Swinging." Ironically, these boys are from two of the richest families in town, and they are planning on robbing his store, but his romantic view of them is distorted by songs that distract him from the danger. Even when he is lying on the floor of the Quik Pik, slowly dying, song lyrics pass through his mind, as if his own death is too hard to imagine without relating it to the trite words of a sad song.

One reviewer compares McCorkle's style in this novel to Flannery O'Connor's, and this accents another difference in McCorkle's second novel. In addition to expanding her point of view, she effectively uses black humor. While humor appears in small doses in *The Cheer Leader,* McCorkle has honed this particular kind of humor to near-perfection in *July 7th.* Charles Husky is murdered after he is robbed; the boys wrap his face with Saran Wrap and leave him to suffocate by the Slurpee machine. Such a scene easily qualifies for this type of humor through its absurdity, inclusion of seemingly insignificant details, and the meaningless of the death. One technique used in black humorous works is the objectification of the victim to create distance between her/him and the audience as a way to ensure that the audience will find the scene amusing rather than sad, and

McCorkle's use of song lyrics helps create the distance necessary to make an amusing scene out of a potentially tragic one.

Songs also play a role in the dreams and illusions of other characters—sometimes humorous but other times almost sentimental in the pathetic references to unmet dreams in life. Fannie McNair listens to gospel music and dreams of a better life for her grandson M.L. Similarly, other characters listen to music that, besides locating the story in a particular era, identifies the defining traits of those characters: Juanita listens to the sentimental "Do You Remember the Times of Your Life" as she reviews her adulterous mistake, and when her efforts to mend her marriage seem successful, she plays Tammy Wynette's "Stand By Your Man." Juvenile delinquent Billy Foster has a poster on his wall of the band KISS, "people with their faces all painted up like some kind of freak show" (20), representative of his own deception as the one who killed Charles Husky. Frances Miller, the Farrah Fawcett lookalike who accidentally runs over the cat, is listening to Olivia Newton-John's "Let's Get Physical," singing the line "I want to get animal, animal" (83). And finally, Sam Swett is reminded of the song Bob Bobbin's name invokes, singing the line which is especially appropriate for Sam: "Wake up, you sleepy head" (165).

Although McCorkle seems to be having a great deal of fun with these songs, their use is not exclusively humorous. In addition to signifying the particular feelings of characters, music can be used as an escape from a life which has not met expectations. Music is an illusion, faster than a movie or book, which takes people away from their daily disappointments. Sam Swett, the reader's guide through Marshboro's seventh of July, claims that he's been trying to explain this aspect of life: "'trying to find lots of answers to a lot of things, struggling to understand society, human nature, to figure out why things are the way that they are instead of the way that we would like to believe they are'" (122). Sam's statement highlights a major theme in *July 7th,* a theme McCorkle will explore many times: what people believe to be the truth is rarely the truth at all.

One last example may help to solidify this theme. Granner Weeks is the one character who everyone acknowledges has a ridiculous fantasy: that is, she believes an Iranian man, Mr. Abdul, has been phoning her constantly to ask her out for pizza. Despite her persistence in telling her story, she says "nobody believes that this man is calling, just because they aren't there when it happens" (32). Her family humors and ignores her. Mr. Abdul, however, may be the only fantasy that is real. After everyone leaves Granner's birthday party, her phone rings, she answers, and it is Mr. Abdul, breathing deeply and wanting to know what she is wearing. If McCorkle wants readers to believe this is fantasy, there is no indication to that effect. The caller appears real, and Granner talks to him for several minutes until he tires of her stories and hangs up. It is no wonder, then, that Granner is the character who thinks, "The damned trouble is that these days nobody knows what's the truth and what ain't" (206).

During the course of the novel, circumstances and people unmask nearly everyone, bluntly laying before Sam and the reader the shame and guilt that fill most people's lives. And while it is clear that truth brings about change and growth in some— Harold and Juanita's marriage will most likely be improved, as will Juanita's relationship with her daughter—McCorkle also suggests that being faced with the truth is not enough per se. Kate and Ernie Stubbs will most likely continue their superficial social climb, and the Fosters will persist in using wealth and power to maintain their image. To illustrate otherwise would be an illusion in itself.

CHAPTER FOUR

Tending to Virginia

Tending to Virginia was published in 1987, three years after McCorkle's first two novels were released. With two such diverse novels setting the tone for her career, critics waited with interest to see with what kind of novel she would follow up the first two, and, generally, they were not disappointed.[1] Diane Manuel of *The Christian Science Monitor* described the new novel as having "multi-dimensional characters [who] put on a show worthy of an Off-Broadway original" as they "argue over and pick at" questions which are "both universal and intimate." *Library Journal* hailed the novel as "an important addition to the works of a promising new writer." But while most of the reviews were positive, some critics seemed to miss the point of the novel; a reviewer in *The New Republic,* for example, criticized the book because "there is no plot worth mentioning," warning readers that they would be "sent into a coma of boredom."[2]

Such caustic words as these last ones would seem to come from a reviewer who expected a traditional plot line with exposition, climax, and denouement, and this is simply not what McCorkle was attempting to create. The novel is a careful character study of four generations of southern women, all related and all seemingly with normal, relatively happy lives. Underneath the thin facade of happiness, though, McCorkle reveals the universal fears, frustrations, dreams, fantasies, and heartaches experienced by women in all cultures and of any generation. The loose plot which defies chronology, however, does make discussion of this novel especially difficult. The best way, perhaps, to get to the heart of the story is through the characters.

The story revolves around Virginia Suzanne Turner Ballard—called Ginny Sue by her hometown friends and family—a twenty-eight-year-old woman who is considering leaving her husband because he kept a secret from her: he divorced his first wife because she intentionally aborted the baby he so wanted. Ginny Sue, seven months pregnant, returns to her hometown of Saxapaw, North Carolina, to consider this revelation, and while there, she develops toxemia and so enjoys the luxury of being "tended to" by her third cousin, mother, aunt, great-aunt, and grandmother—all strong, independent women, but all withholding secrets from each other and living lives that have required more than a few compromises.

Although McCorkle was not yet a mother when she wrote this book, she based this novel on bits and pieces of family stories. She told one reviewer that "the novel's preoccupation with the power and pull of collective memories reflects her own. 'The question is, how do you hold on and still move on?'"[3] How, indeed? The answer McCorkle offers differs from character to character, and the reader is left knowing that no two lives are the same and that no two people will face or solve their problems in the same way.

Tending to Virginia is divided into seven sections—resembling seven scenes in a stage play. Most sections are divided into much smaller sections from several pages long to just a paragraph. McCorkle uses third-person limited point of view, with each smaller section told through the eyes of a different character. What comes from this structuring using multiple points of view is a variety of stories in a style reminiscent of William Faulkner. Sometimes the same story is told by several different characters, and sometimes only parts of stories are told, leaving details to be added later in the novel. The result of this loosely constructed, conversation-driven plot is an honest portrayal of real women. Little by little, as in real life, readers see—through monologues, memories, flashbacks, and conversations—the characters as individuals, not only mother and grandmother and cousin, but Hannah and Emily and Madge, women who have not always been defined and limited by their roles in life and relationships with others.

There are two family trees listed in the book before one word of the story is told. McCorkle graphs a maternal family tree consisting of the characters in the novel: Virginia Suzanne White (Ginny Sue's great-grandmother), her two daughters and one daughter-in-law (Lena, Emily, and Tessy), their daughters (Madge and Hannah), and the next generation (Cindy and Ginny Sue). Husbands, brothers, and sons are listed, but only as a reference; the family line is clearly matriarchal. In addition, McCorkle dedicates her book to her own family tree. She writes the book "In Memory of *Claudia Meares Bullington*" (her grandmother's sister) and "*With love for: Margaret Ann (Annie) Meares Collins, Melba Collins McCorkle, Jan McCorkle Gane and Margaret Ann (Annie) Gane*" (respectively her grandmother, her mother, her sister, and her niece). By restructuring her own family tree, making it matriarchal, McCorkle focuses the attention of readers on the female life and voice, identifying it as equally significant in the life of a woman, if not more so, than the patriarchal line.

As the novel's epigraph, McCorkle uses lines from Mary Shelley's *Frankenstein:* "Thus strangely are our souls constructed and by such slight ligaments are we bound to prosperity or ruin." This quotation accents several ideas in the novel. First, it draws attention to the arbitrary—almost accidental—manner in which many of the most important decisions in life such as marriage and children are made, an idea which will be very significant in the stories the characters tell. Second, Shelley's lines point out the fragility of the bindings which tie people to each other, to sanity and health, and to life itself, and as the novel illustrates, for women these frail connections are often dependent upon men—as fathers, as husbands, as lovers.

Fear is a major hindrance to the women in this novel: they fear change, they fear loneliness, they fear failure in marriage and motherhood. These fears have driven them to keep secrets from each other, presenting instead a facade of contentment. All of the women, in their attempts to avoid the things they fear, have settled for less than the ideal, but it is not until they gather together around Ginny Sue's bed during a thunderstorm one afternoon that they finally reveal to each other their true inner selves, their wishes, their disappointments and regrets, and their guilt. These revelations support one of McCorkle's major themes as mentioned earlier: What people believe to be true is probably not true at all, and more often people lie to the ones they love to maintain the mask of falsehoods, believing others are exactly what they seem. Despite a few confidences shared, it is surprising how little of the truth these women, who claim to be so close, have told each other. The scene during the storm, covering about fifteen pages, is filled with numerous statements of awakening, surprise, and resentment such as "I didn't know that either. . . . I was never told anything," "That's a lie," and "I can't believe you didn't tell me" (230–51). McCorkle suggests here that the people we claim to know best are, in fact, strangers in many ways because we fear hurting or disappointing them by sharing the truth about our weaknesses.

In section 1 McCorkle introduces Ginny Sue, living in a rented house with her law student husband, Mark, feeling grossly unattractive and "barefoot and pregnant and hot as hell" (4). Most important, though, Ginny is struggling with the news that her husband left his first wife because she had an abortion. Ginny, it seems, has not even told her family that Mark was married before, and so this newest revelation weighs on her as heavily as the baby in her womb, which she fears will soon "bust out and take control of her life" (5). Life seems too ephemeral to Ginny and she yearns for something solid and permanent: "the rented house, temporary, temporary, a temporary life; pregnancy is temporary" (10). Ginny's fear of the future is most certainly fear of change. As she rocks in a rocking chair—symbolic of movement that keeps her in the same place—she focuses on the instability of life: "[A]ll those years, the bits and pieces that she can't get off her mind, and then it started changing, one thing after another; Gram's move to the duplex, a Piggly Wiggly replacing Gram's old house, Raymond's suicide, Roy dying, Lena having to move to a home, Cindy divorced remarried and divorced again, and Gram's hair turning so white, her mind wandering back and forth over the years" (33, 34). Resistant to any change because it demands she be more independent and flexible, Ginny lets her fears escalate as she considers the future. She fears moving even farther away from her family. (Mark is planning to move the family to Richmond, Virginia, as soon as his schooling is finished.) Like many people her age, Ginny wants the security of a house and family around her, not realizing yet that every woman has to make the transition from the home of her childhood, where she is cared for, to the home where she is the parent, where she must be the caretaker. McCorkle repeats the scene of women making this transition throughout the novel in flashbacks and memories of the other women in Ginny's family, helping Ginny to understand the universality of this transition.

The major mistake Ginny makes is equating the physical home with an emotional one. Linda Tate, in *A Southern Weave of Women,* notes that "McCorkle inextricably fuses ideas of home and family." To Ginny, home is a place, a building, a geographical location, and she dreams of returning to her home "where history and knowledge is solid" (17). Eventually, though, she learns to see home as a situation which includes the people she loves, no matter where they may be geographically, and just because, for example, her grandmother's old house has been torn down and replaced with a Piggly Wiggly, "home" is still intact. Tate also points out that as Ginny grows in her understanding of home; in "one of the title's several meanings, then, Virginia is 'tending to Virginia,' that is, moving tentatively away from North Carolina and toward Virginia," where she and her husband will establish their own home.[4]

Perhaps more than anything else, Ginny feels angry. Throughout the first section Ginny expresses anger over both simple things, such as "people that she barely knows who think they have some right to walk up and pat her stomach like it might be a dog" (8), and more serious issues, including what she perceives as her husband's betrayal of trust by not telling her the truth about the breakup of his first marriage and her belief that she is merely "the substitute" wife who will bear him the child he desires (16). Her anger manifests itself in the mural she paints on the nursery wall. She begins with the idea of an Animal Kingdom with "tame gentle animals with cute little faces like Care Bears and Peppi Le Peu," but she paints instead serpents and vultures and alligators (15). The walls of the nursery are reminiscent of the wallpaper in Charlotte Perkins Gilman's short story "The Yellow Wallpaper" (1891). Like the unnamed narrator of Gilman's story who is suffering from depression brought on by childbirth which eventually leads to her total emotional and psychological breakdown, Ginny is sad and angry and thinking crazy thoughts. Her nursery is yellow, too, and ,like the room in Gilman's tale, feels more like a prison than a place of rest and happiness. In contrast to the cheery connotation most people give to the color, Ginny "hates yellow" and "wishes there was absolutely nothing yellow in the entire world" (11). Near the end of the novel, as Ginny approaches her realization that all women have felt as she does and wanted to run back to the security of mother and home, the room at her grandmother's duplex takes on "a strange yellow glow" from the "yellow sky" outside (256). In one significant scene, Ginny's grandmother, Emily, tells her story of leaving her husband and running home to her mother. When her mother wisely sends Emily back to her husband, she walks home, and "the sky looked yellow" (277). Yellow here is symbolic of fear and of isolation, of too much sudden responsibility and of a lack of understanding about a new role in life, much like the yellow in Gilman's short story.

Ginny's talent in painting is tied as well to the illusion/reality theme in this novel. When Ginny was in high school, her art teacher, Mrs. Abbott, nicknamed her "little Monet," convincing Ginny that she had talent, a belief that directed her education and career as a grade school art teacher. She believed then that she "was special, thought she was the first, thought she had been given a name because she was good and different from the rest" (38). Years later, Ginny finds herself standing in front of a Monet exhibit, startled and astounded by Monet's greatness, and she comments: "Mrs. Abbot did not tell the whole truth—a lie, deception. . . . Her face flushed with inadequacy while reality burst forth, *you will never in your life do anything that can compare*" (38). This is perhaps the first time Ginny realizes that the lies people tell—even though they are meant to protect and bolster others—can be injurious and manipulative, for Ginny believes if she had known the truth about her "talent," she "would have majored in something else and been a consultant instead of knotting knots and getting frustrated with sixth graders" (38).

One other painting by Ginny plays an important role in the extension of McCorkle's theme of change—of the inability of people to stop change from occurring despite their fear. Ginny paints a picture of Saxapaw with the old and the new both represented. The old Saxapaw includes two black men playing horseshoes outside an old establishment called Cutty's Place near the railroad tracks. She juxtaposes this scene with "condos, rigid brick structures with a yardful of dirt, no trees, miniblinds . . . a Trailways bus sign, small brick building, a Coke machine." She describes the "old part and the new part, until the old finally fell away. The old family farms, fields and sky, distorted by a bright red and yellow Burger King sign" (160–61). By contrasting the old with the new South, McCorkle illustrates that it is impossible to stop what is seen as progress, that change is inevitable, and that the survivors will be the ones who can adjust to it.

Connected to the idea of painting, photographs again become important in extending the theme of illusion and misperception. Much like Jo Spencer in *The Cheer Leader,* Ginny is drawn to photographs because they "freeze" time, much in the same way she is pulled toward Saxapaw, where "everything is just the same, always the same" (99). Photographs seem so real to Ginny that she even turns "her back to all of the photographs on the dresser" when she changes clothes (41). She craves the stability photos represent, but at the same time they force her to acknowledge people and events she would rather forget. For example, when Ginny's first engagement is broken, she "stood right out there in the backyard and poured lighter fluid on the wedding portrait, lit a match" (73), as if she could erase the past simply by destroying tangible evidence that it had existed. Despite their ability—seemingly—to freeze moments, however, McCorkle illustrates that photographs are, at the same time, open to interpretation. In a dream Ginny has on the first page of the novel, she imagines a photograph of her grandmother Emily, with her grandmother's sister, Lena. The sisters are sitting on the front porch during the summer after the death of Emily's baby, and in Ginny's mind the picture comes to life with movement, sound, and color. She hears them describe the summer from their separate points of view:

> "Lena thought I needed her company the summer my baby died," Gram said. "I didn't have the heart to tell her there was nothing anybody could do."
> Lena said, "Emily needed me all that summer. I couldn't go back to New York with her that way. It was like I was her mama." (3)

Along with the idea that photographs are open to interpretation—as Ginny's imagination illustrates—this scene also shows how the same situation can be perceived in a completely different way by different people. To both Lena and Emily, what they say is the truth, but neither perception is completely accurate.

The idea that photographs are not fixed both disturbs and pleases Ginny. In her jealousy about Mark's first wife, Sheila, Ginny refashions their life together based on the "too small, too blurred" wedding photo she has seen, envisioning a woman far superior to herself and every other woman. She constructs an elaborate identity for Sheila and hears her voice coming from the picture: "I jog and I play tennis and I go to the spa to work out and do aerobics three times a week and I only watch PBS, never anything other than PBS, and I never have PMS" (36). With such unreal expectations and unfair comparisons, it is no wonder that Ginny feels inadequate in her marriage. She pictures Sheila as hovering "like the cobweb in the corner, ready to wrap and twist and strangle their life like a cord around a neck" (139). This imagery connects Sheila to the abortion she had as well as gives Ginny the justification to leave her husband and return home, where she is "safe" and everyone loves her in spite of her shortcomings.

When Ginny does run home and is surrounded by the women of her family, she hears their stories and finds she is not alone in her fears and doubts and sadness. McCorkle seems to be suggesting that the life of a woman is difficult, but that true growth comes in the endurance. Madge Pearson is the last of the group to tell her secrets, but her story is the most shocking and extreme. Madge reveals that she did love her husband Raymond when she married him, that he made her happy, but sometime later he changed drastically as mental illness turned him into a person Madge hardly recognized, a person who somehow convinced Madge to help him kill himself by pulling the trigger of the gun he held to his chest. This harrowing scene is the culmination of many years of suffering for Madge. McCorkle carefully builds an insanity case against this man who had a King Tut fixation in conjunction with an obsession about death and preservation in death. In keeping with the theme of reality masked by illusion, most of Raymond's eccentricities occur in private. He forces Madge to separate and seal his underwear and socks in new airtight baggies, and he once asks Madge to "soak in a cool bath and then lay real still on the bed" (82). He watches his mother-in-law being embalmed in the funeral home and seems pleased by it, and in one mummy-like reference, Madge describes watching him wrap a dead bird in toilet paper.

At various times, however, Raymond's abnormalities become public, and it is on these occasions when Madge feels most horrified. In the most extreme situation, Raymond climbs "'on the roof of Kinglee Hardware with his eyes all made up like a woman, blue shadow and long black eyeliner tails, "Like Tut," he said'" (79). He also plays terrifying games with his daughter—and later Ginny, as she narrates: "'He told me that I'd look nice in a tomb,' Virginia whispers. 'He said he could just see me wrapped up in a pure white sheet, my body oiled and perfumed, and he made me tell him that he was the king, that he was beautiful and that I worshipped him, and he said that I better never tell that I said all of those things to him because everyone would hate me'" (242). Finally, he asks to be buried in a huge vault with all of his favorite possessions, including a brand new wide-screen television set, much as the Egyptians were buried with their treasures. Raymond is both scared of and drawn to death, and the peace and serenity found in death, coupled with the security of believing life will go on in another realm, is seductive to him. One might even say that he has a death wish, finally fulfilled by his wife.

The role of photographs again becomes important in the story of Madge and Raymond. Once Raymond dies, Madge admits to herself that she "would like to burn that picture [of Raymond], and when she's alone she turns it face down so that he can't see what she's doing" (110). Madge also remembers asking Raymond if he has any pictures of his relatives, to which Raymond answers, "No pictures. . . . They're all dead" (129). Similar to Ginny's open interpretation of photographs, it is immaterial whether his relatives are actually dead; he has made them dead by destroying any pictures, re-creating his past according to his own wishes.

Ginny's memory of her terrifying encounter with Raymond is pivotal in the development of her fears. McCorkle replays the scene several times in the novel, each time offering more information and detail. In short, Ginny is upstairs alone at Madge and Raymond's home, and Raymond arrives home and comes slowly and frighteningly up the stairs, wearing a mask. He wants Ginny to let him wrap her in a sheet and wants her to tell him she worships him, but she resists. He threatens to kill her if she tells anyone. In a moment of frustration, Raymond throws a hairbrush and breaks a mirror, and when other family members arrive, he blames the broken mirror on Ginny, who is too afraid to say anything. The breaking of the mirror surfaces many times in the memory of Ginny and seems quite significant. In a nod toward Lacan's mirror stage of development, McCorkle accomplishes at least two things with this incident. First, it symbolizes the shattering of Raymond's cohesive self. In Ginny's eyes, she finally sees this man as splintered into more than just the uncle she knew. Second, Ginny's identity is forever marred by this encounter. After this day, she is afraid—afraid that others will not believe her and hate her if she tells the truth, afraid of her uncle, and especially afraid to be alone. It is probably the first time that Ginny sees herself as a vulnerable and objectified self, and it affects her relationships with men later in her life.

Ginny is not the only woman filled with the fear of being alone. McCorkle intersperses into the story similar memories of the other women in the family. The women attempt to fill the void of loneliness by various means. Lena, who cannot have children, fills her house with cats. Some women, such as Hannah, fill their lives with children or work. Cindy attempts to assuage her loneliness with a string of noncommittal, worthless men, which, she says, is "'better than being alone'" (183). Ginny's grandmother reminds her that when "'you're lying in your bed at night, God is there with you'" (181), and Madge plays solitaire, keeping track of the debt she owes the imaginary dealer. But the women are still lonely, and McCorkle suggests that until women stop looking for an end to their loneliness in men and turn to other women for support, they will continue to be lonely. Several of the women are widows, and through them McCorkle illustrates that even good marriages will eventually end in death, and if a man is all a woman has, she will then be lonely. As Linda Tate points out, the women in this novel "continue to define themselves in terms of family" instead of as individuals, persisting in seeing themselves in terms of the men in their lives and their identities as wives, mothers, and lovers.[5]

In contrast to Ginny's marriage to Mark—which seems relatively good, despite her current misgivings—McCorkle offers Cindy, a woman with two failed marriages who is currently seeing a married man whom she met at happy hour at the local Ramada Inn. Cindy is an example of the alter ego McCorkle often creates for her protagonist—a character sometimes too confident for her own good. She is oversexed, fixated on her father, frustrated by her situation, and, above all, angry. (She uses forms of the phrase "pissed off" no less than nine times in a ten-page stretch.) But she is a survivor, and while

Ginny lies passively in her bed, letting the women in her family tend to her every need while she internally whines over her husband's first marriage, Cindy is taking action to improve her life. She is looking for the next "Mr. Cindy" and has developed a pragmatic attitude for life: "Just put your quarter in one of those machines and get what you never in your life wanted but take it and live with it. Bodies are like that, those little clear plastic eggs, and you take what's good out of it, a red rubber worm or a fake diamond ring and then throw that little egg in the trash" (126). Her jealousy about her first ex-husband's new fiancée parallels Ginny's jealousy over Sheila, both situations appearing pointless and childish—but realistic. Cindy is far from ideal—especially in her understanding about the place of men in women's lives—but McCorkle uses her as a foil for Ginny, suggesting the best life lies somewhere in between.

Men and the roles they play in women's lives is an important and yet perplexing issue in this novel, and McCorkle offers no easy answer to the conflict between need for love and need for independence. On one hand, as Cindy points out, "Everybody really does need a man there to help them" (191), and some women do not understand "what a difference a little manly attention can make in this otherwise suck hole world" (219). On the other hand, as the women come together and share their secrets and grow more intimate, they express such thoughts as "Children, parents, men, and life will kick you right in the teeth and you best get used to it, learn to live with it" (265). What are readers to make of these contradictory statements?

Two minor characters in the novel may hold the key to this dilemma. First is Felicia, Emily's neighbor who is believed to be a lesbian. Ostensibly, the women in Ginny's family disapprove of Felicia's sexual orientation—as well as misunderstand it. As Madge is reviewing the wreckage of her marriage to Raymond, she makes several comments suggesting a kind of jealousy of Felicia's freedom to live without men. Her first comment hedges a bit: "Sometimes, Madge can almost see why Felicia chose her way, life without men." Her next comment, though, reveals more envy than anything else: "Felicia has probably never had a man that made her do something she didn't want to do." Later, thinking with relief about her independence as a widow, she "watches Felicia pulling weeds and she is relieved it's all over" (194–96). At this point, she has connected Felicia's life without men to her own life without Raymond, and despite her early love for him, she prefers loneliness over subjugation and fear. Felicia becomes a symbol for these women of what they would be without men, and the image is not altogether disturbing. They are, perhaps, envious of her strength and independence, but they are unable to admit that, even to themselves.

The other woman who plays a major role in the debate over loneliness versus marriage is already dead at the time of the Ginny's stay in Saxapaw: Tessy, Lena and Emily's sister-in-law. Tessy's presence, however, is keenly felt throughout the novel in memory and conversation. She represents the worst of women's lives: a life virtually devoid of choice. Married at age thirteen to thirty-year-old Harv Pearson, she turns to her new sister-in-law Emily on her wedding day: "Tessy was not but thirteen with eyes like saucers, knowing she was going to have to climb in bed with a man she barely knew when the sun went down and Harv come up from that field. 'I'm so scared,' she had whispered to Emily. 'I know there ain't a God for this to happen to me'" (230). Nine pregnancies, including three miscarriages, define Tessy's married life as well as years marked by hard work with little compensation for a lost childhood. There are three incidents, however, which bring her story life and meaning and influence the lives of the other women in the novel. The first concerns a dogwood tree that Hannah plants on the day Tessy dies, naming it after Tessy. The dogwood tree, McCorkle explains, is "a symbol of resurrection in that cross pattern and little blood-pink marks" (283), especially significant considering Tessy's earlier comment that there is no God and a later one in which she asks, "'What kind of God makes a woman live like me?'" (129). Tessy appears to have changed her mind about God and about her seemingly unhappy life. Two other events may be responsible for her change of heart. One of the family secrets is that Tessy fell in love with a man named Jake who occasionally taught violin in Saxapaw. Even though nothing long-term came of the love between them—and McCorkle hints that they might have consummated their love only one time—just his presence in Tessy's life makes it a life worth living. After Tessy sees him and experiences joy for perhaps the first time, McCorkle remarks that "Tessy feels stronger now; she feels the energy coming back to her, she hears that slow sweet tune with every step of her feet in those dead crackly leaves." When Emily encourages her to ask God for forgiveness, Tessy answers, "'I ain't so sure I want to be forgiven; that's asking forgiveness for the best part of my life'" (297–300).

Such a message of guiltless love found any way possible is interesting and a bit shocking—if it were not for one other incident McCorkle describes from Tessy's life. When Harv was a young man, he had had an accident with an ax that left a crescent-shaped white scar on his shin. During her middle-aged years—long after the fiddler had left town—Tessy finds herself one night lifting the leg of his pajamas to see the scar while Harv continues to sleep. For the first time in their marriage, she touches it tenderly, kissing it, caressing it. An awareness of Harv's "flesh and blood," of his humanness comes to her, and she thinks the words she has never said: "I love you, Harv." This scene recurs many times in the coming months, and she often cries as she looks at the scar. This scar, the symbol of Harv's vulnerability and of her lost innocence in childhood, is the first and only connection Tessy ever makes with Harv. It suggests the difficulty of women's lives but that the ability to transcend hardship with love and connection means survival and even a sort of happiness.

In contrast to the often miserable marriages of Tessy, Madge, and Cindy, McCorkle offers three women with seemingly happy marriages: Lena, Emily, and Hannah. But in keeping with her theme of illusion versus reality, all is not as it seems. Overall, the women are happy, but their lives are far from perfect. Lena's grief over not being able to have children has haunted her whole marriage, and regardless of how many cats she and Roy adopt, there is still a gap which cannot be filled. In addition, after Roy dies, she is angry with him for leaving her—so mad that she refuses to attend his funeral. When she develops Alzheimer's, she moves to a nursing home, and "all that was left of Lena's life was in a Samsonite bag and a pasteboard box" (33). At the nursing home, she finds herself confused and scared, holding onto a baby doll for comfort. Emily, too, is suffering from Alzheimer's, and the real tragedy of her disease and Lena's is that they have so much good advice to share with the younger generations, but they are unable to communicate it in any sensible way. Much like the younger women who fail to communicate out of fear, these women are also victims, forced to keep too many secrets and lies. When Cindy comments about Emily and Lena, "Deception and hallucination, both common to Alzheimer's disease," her words take on double meaning: deception and illusion have certainly ruled the lives of all the women in this tale, regardless of health.

Hannah and Emily, however, have had as good a life as possible. Emily expresses a real love for her husband, James, and seems sincerely despondent about his death. Hannah is a woman who lives "day to day and year to year" (74), content to trade Lena's real lights of Broadway for romantic movies and the adventure of travel for Ben, the boring but good man she married. She loves her husband and fears the time when she, too, will be alone like her mother and aunt, but McCorkle seems to propose that this is the price for love and happiness— and that it is worth it.

Throughout the novel McCorkle uses blood imagery, often associated with women because of the menstrual cycle, to represent women and their ties to each other—through the literal blood which flows through their related bodies and to the mark of blood that all women share. But the imagery also illustrates the lack of communication between the women because of fear: they allow other women to "bleed" both literally and figuratively rather than break a code of silence brought on by insecurity and fear of exposure. The first time blood plays a part in the plot is the beginning of Ginny's illness, when she sits down on the bathroom floor to avoid fainting and notices that she is bleeding. Unfortunately, the only two people who are there to help are the two women suffering from Alzheimer's disease. They confuse her toxemia with having her period, telling her "'it's not the kind of thing to discuss'" (104). As her fear and frustration mount, she is unable to communicate any better than the two older women. Finally, Emily calls Felicia and asks for a Kotex, and Felicia immediately comes over to help. Later on, Emily brings up Ginny's bleeding again, sure it is her "time of the month," and reminds the other women several times, "'We never discussed such'" and "I wouldn't discuss it'" (165–66). This leads Hannah to an observation that she had to learn about sex from Madge—which elicits the response from Emily, "'Madge shouldn't have told.'"

Such secrecy between women about an important subject in their lives is both debilitating and tragic. It leads to scenes such as the one described by Lena in the final section. She remembers thinking "she's dying at thirteen" when she first sees blood on her underwear. She prays, asks forgiveness for sins, and feels confused and scared. The only situations she can compare it to are those she's seen men experience: Harv's ax accident and the murder of a black man—neither of which makes sense to her in terms of her own bleeding. When she finally tells her mother she is dying, her mother looks at her "as if she's done something wrong in not knowing" and tells her "how women are put on this earth to suffer, that it is God's will that they suffer" (301–2). Lena's fear, anger, and confusion could have been easily avoided through communication—by women sharing with each other. And yet the fear of being honest is exactly what keeps women in ignorance generation after generation.

In the modern setting of the novel, McCorkle demonstrates just how far the newest generation has come. In a scene filled with scatological humor, Cindy believes she has lost a tampon inside her, and so she runs to Ginny and Madge for help. This leads to an animated discussion of what a woman should and should not do during "that time." The embarrassment of the old generation juxtaposed with the nonchalance of Ginny and Cindy is notable. Perhaps it is McCorkle's way of signaling that the newest woman of the South will not play the silence game anymore; both Cindy and Ginny are Women of the New South in the truest sense of the phrase. They instinctively know that breaking communication barriers is the key to knowledge, and knowledge—of self, of one's own body—is power.

Related to the blood imagery is the image of motherhood. As Tate notes, "Mothering—participating in the propagation of the family network—permeates the novel."[6] Along with menstrual blood—and the stoppage of it during pregnancy—McCorkle fills the novel with maternal semblances. Pregnancy, blood, sexuality, love, and the "womb" of Ginny's grandmother's house all mark the maternal world as significant. All these women need to be mothered—long after they have become mothers themselves. The transition from child to mother is an abrupt one, and one for which women are perhaps not adequately prepared. As Emily remarks to Ginny, "'Sometimes I feel so alone and what I'm lonely for is my mother'" (181). Ginny, overwhelmed with her approaching motherhood and fearing that the child will take over her life and force her to be the caretaker instead of the one being cared for, experiences the same sensation as Emily and so runs home to the one place she can still be a child. It is through a week of hearing similar stories of women successfully making the transition from child to mother that she gains the strength to return to Mark and make her own home.

Section 5 of the novel takes place during a storm and electrical outage, representative of the turbulence and lack of vision these women have experienced. Within this section most of the secrets are revealed. As section 6 begins, the storm has passed, and a cleansing rain falls, symbolizing the opportunity for a fresh start these women can have if they turn to one another. They have been wearing masks with the intention of protecting each other, when actually it is the truth which literally sets them free from fear and guilt. Images of death, emptiness, loss, and barrenness in earlier sections are replaced with images typifying light, ripeness, growth, and community. Madge, released from guilt by the other women, is the character who seems the most changed, but other characters go through similar transitions. In section 7 the women, both dead and alive, come to terms with their marriages and the men with whom they share their lives. It is the section in which the dogwood symbolism is explained, in which Tessy touches Harv's scar, in which women remember losing husbands, sons, and brothers but still survive. It is also the section in which the matriarch of the family—Virginia Suzanne Pearson—appears. She is the woman from whom all the others in this story spring, and yet in the two sections which describe her life, it is obvious that her life was no better than any other woman's, filled with both pain and joy—symbolized by the pain of giving birth followed by the joy of holding the newborn baby.

Good coming from pain is one of the major themes in this book. In the final section McCorkle ascribes to various characters lines which lead readers to an understanding of how all these stories weave together to bring wisdom. To Ginny, Emily repeats several times what her mother told her: "'you got to learn to let go, Emily. God taught me with that thunderstorm that you just got to let go'" (275). Ginny's grandmother is not telling her to separate from her family so much as to extend the family with her own. In a dream Ginny describes at the beginning of section 7, she sees herself with a "full belly" contrasted within a land that is "sterile" and full of "emptiness." Images of overripe corn are stark against "one perfect ear" of corn, and she imagines her hair "tied and knotted" with the silk—perhaps as an indication of marriage. Symbols of light and dark, death and ripeness, oppose each other as she makes her way into her grandmother's house. Suddenly she notices that her belly is flat and she asks her grandmother where her baby is. Her grandmother's words are simple: "'We all lose things, Ginny Sue. We hold on so tight and we lose them just the same'" (281–83). Scenes such as this one are what keep the ending of this novel from becoming maudlin. Yes, the women have come far in their honesty with each other, and McCorkle indicates that the future will be different for them because of the changes they have made, but for every gain there is a loss, and as Ginny's dream points out, all things must pass and die—no matter how hard people hold onto them. The cycles of birth and death, love and loss, are inescapable, and it is this lesson that Ginny finally learns after hearing stories told by other women. At the end of the novel, Ginny's baby has not been born—and perhaps that would have been too formulaic in this realistic novel—but, of course, the birth is inevitable, as is that baby's own growth, loss of innocence, separation from mother, and movement to a home of his/her own.

The final few pages of *Tending to Virginia* depict Ginny as eager to return home, and most important, she has a vision for what she wants to paint on the walls of her baby's nursery. She remembers clearly a scene from her childhood showing her hometown as it was then. Her painting—which is her story—will be her gift to her child in the same way that the stories she has heard during her week of "tending" were the gift she received. She is focused on the future, and as it begins to rain, she thinks of the clouds "letting go" much in the same way she is letting go—and yet, in her memory, she thinks of a time when her grandmother told her she will "always be with" her (312). The images of renewing rain, flowing rivers, and ripe corn in the final paragraph prepare readers for Ginny Sue's future: she can be a separate individual yet still be connected to her past.

CHAPTER FIVE

Ferris Beach

When McCorkle set out to write her fourth novel, her inspiration was her childhood interest in Anne Frank. She wanted to write about a modern day "hiding out" situation, perhaps a young girl who runs away from her family and spends a summer with a wayward relative. The young girl's experiences would teach her about "accepting what is true. That what appears to be true is *not*."[1] Recognizing truth becomes the most important idea in the novel, as it is in so many of McCorkle's works. The reviews of the novel, *Ferris Beach,* were overwhelmingly favorable. *The New York Times Book Review* reported that "Jill McCorkle is a writer who has delivered on her earlier promise—and who promises still more," and *The Atlanta Journal and Constitution* asserted that she "digs deeper and uncovers new levels of understanding with each book." Great praise was given for McCorkle's use of voice in this novel—as accurate, captivating, and "so strong and clear"—as well as for her "deft comic sense."[2] Indeed, her literary reputation was building with each novel, and her reviews were found in more prominent journals and on earlier pages within them.

In *Ferris Beach,* published in 1990, McCorkle returns to both the structure and subject of her first novel, *The Cheer Leader.* Again the narrator is a young girl growing up in a small southern town: Fulton, North Carolina. The major difference between Jo Spencer and the narrator of *Ferris Beach,* Kate Burns, is that, superficially, Jo appears to have it all, to have and be what every young girl would desire, when in fact she is hiding her insecurities under a fragile facade. Kate, on the other hand, wears her vulnerability on her face—a wine-colored, Italy-shaped birthmark—her "weak spot, like a bruise."[3] Whenever she feels embarrassed or humiliated or frightened, Kate's fingers instinctively reach up to cover the mark protectively.

Ferris Beach is a female bildungsroman of the most classic kind. Kate moves from innocence to experience, from childish illusion to mature realization, and from ignorance about romance and sex to an understanding of true love and acceptance. Like many of McCorkle's characters, Kate fills her life with lies and self-delusion, misinterpreting the world because of the stories she has been told as a child, and she must shed these illusions before she can move from childhood to adulthood. Many of her misconceptions are regional trappings, and as a southern novel, *Ferris Beach* makes a satirical comment on the culture in which Kate is raised. In the New South, regional history and family stories have become less important to children and young adults such as Kate than popular culture has, specifically movies, music, and television. Although Kate's mother—a Yankee who nonetheless recognizes the advantages of being part of southern society—encourages and even forces Kate to participate in groups such as the Children of the Confederacy, these types of activities are targets for mockery from Kate and her friend Misty. A neighbor, Mrs. Poole, represents the traditional Old South, and McCorkle consistently presents her satirically, clinging to her outdated rules of behavior such as smoking only while sitting with a roof over her head and blaming all the misfortunes of the town on the building of split-level homes. Mrs. Poole, writes McCorkle, "could see no merit in *any* changes, whether it was the Coca-Cola bottle getting taller or Mo Rhodes turning the yard of her split-level into a Japanese garden, or black children walking the halls of Samuel T. Saxon Junior High" (43). Her refusal to consider that change can be positive marks her as unsuitable in today's South, a deterrent to forward movement because she is averse to movement of any kind.

Although Kate's family lives next to the Whispering Pines Cemetery, it is not a place to learn history and honor the dead; it has become the spot for young people to meet and have sex, and Kate's walks through the cemetery enlighten her not about the past but about condoms. Kate's expectations about life are defined not by history but by popular culture. The first time a boy holds Kate's hand, she can relate her feelings and her actions only to lines from current songs: "Have You Seen Her?" and *"Did you write the book of love?"* and *"Hold me like you'll never let me go."* Her only understanding of love is what she has heard in songs, read in books such as *Valley of the Dolls,* and seen in movies such as *Stella Dallas, Madame X,* and *Imitation of Life.* Self-image for Misty and Kate is determined by attitudes, actions, and clothing found in *Glamour* magazine and from television shows of the early 1970s such as *That Girl* and *Maude* (77–80). Most of the residents of Fulton, it seems, have exchanged their loyalties from the past to the present. Misty's mother, Mo Rhodes, names her new baby "Buddy" after the singer Buddy Holly (122). Ironically, she believes in "naming after the dead," but instead of choosing a family name, she chooses a name from popular culture. Sally Jean Rhodes, who eventually becomes Misty's stepmother, is also tied more to the icons of today than the heroes of yesterday: "Sally had once seen Liberace in an airport, and she used this as a way to mark all of the events of her life"—either before or after this seemingly most important moment of her existence (125).

With childish romantic illusions propagated by movies, music, and television, it is no wonder that Kate's understanding of love is superficial and idealistic. As a female bildungsroman, the novel follows Kate's psychological journey as she discovers the many and varied faces of love. As a child Kate has read the biography of Helen Keller nine times, pretending in blindfolded simulation to be Keller, "wandering around [her] room and spelling words into [her] own hand" (1). The Helen Keller game is tied to several other motifs in the book; first, this self-imposed blindness is tied to Kate's feelings of vulnerability because of her birthmark. By imagining a worse handicap, she can minimize her pain and realize that "a little birthmark is NOT the end of the world" (25). In addition, the game suggests that she cannot—or prefers not to—see what is real and what is not. Kate invents the game one night when she hears her parents arguing about the irresponsible behavior of her father's niece Angela. Because of her attachment to and idealization of Angela, Kate simply shuts out the truth by pretending to be deaf and blind. As Kate develops and accepts the truth about Angela and other people as well, her childish game of blindness and the attachment to Helen Keller disappear.

Angela is not the only character who is idealized by Kate. In fact, the book can be seen as a female heroic quest in search of the mother figure. As Carol Pearson and Katherine Pope point out in their study, *The Female Hero in American Literature,* female heroes, like male heroes, must reject the status quo and tradition-ally held beliefs—represented by mother and home—before they can discover truth, recognize potential, and reconcile with the dominant culture. But unlike male heroes, female heroes do not finally dominate or control their world; instead they master the world by understanding it.[4] In southern culture this understanding has in the past been accompanied by relegation to a powerless position in the male-dominated society, but recent literature has demonstrated a change in this pattern, and more often the realiza-tion includes self-empowerment and also reconciliation with the mother who was previously rejected.

In *Ferris Beach* Kate follows this pattern very closely. From the beginning Kate rejects her mother and looks for a replacement, finding candidates in community and extended family. But as her illusions about womanhood are shattered one by one, Kate watches her idols slip off the unsteady pedestals she has constructed, and she is left with little to support her fan-tasies. Unlike Jo Spencer in *The Cheer Leader*—who finds support and identity through her family—Kate rejects her mother and the identity she represents. To separate her own identity from her mother's, Kate practices a form of "self-orphaning." In keeping with the link to current rather than his-torical times, self-orphaning is especially important to southern females because by rejecting their family names and identities, as Joan Schultz has observed, "they signal themselves as resist-ing, refusing, or rejecting the kind of family identity, family roles, and family ties with the past or the present considered so vital to the Southern way of life."[5] And although Cleva is a displaced Yankee, she has deliberately set out to initiate her daughter into southern traditions, knowing the importance of connections in a southern community.

In an attempt to define herself as Not-Cleva's-Daughter, Kate imagines herself as the Little Match Girl, rescued from orphanhood by Angela (who was herself an orphan), believing and hoping that she is Angela's "love child" (3–4). Instead of her own mother, Kate claims she would "rather take [her] chances drawing a mother out of a hat" (54). Several of the movies she watches over and over—such as *Stella Dallas* and *Madame X*—are about mothers who are forced to leave their children to be raised by other people, and Kate creates an elaborate fantasy about her orphanhood and the cover-up. Having once rejected her mother—and perhaps the traditional southern ideals her mother has tried to instill within her—Kate begins her quest for a more "suitable" mother figure. She chooses three females, all representing idealized female status and behavior as Kate understands it at her young age. Although all three females are southern by birth, they each have rejected the southern woman's role in some way, ending up on the margins of proper southern society.

The first woman on Kate's list of ideal mothers is her father's niece Angela. Angela is the family's recurrent prodigal daughter, irresponsible with money and unlucky in love. Kate is only five years old when she first meets Angela; knowing that Cleva does not approve of Angela, Kate's father secretly takes her to meet Angela at Ferris Beach. It is during this first meeting that Angela and Ferris Beach both attain icon status, representing everything that is beautiful and romantic to naive

Kate. It is a powerful memory for many reasons, not the least of which is that it is the first time she consciously deceives her mother—a scene she will reenact later in the novel during her first sexual experience—but also, her description of the moment is steeped in romantic language, words which reveal the depth of Kate's illusions about both the woman and the place: "It was that very day that I attached to Angela everything beautiful and lively and good; she was the easy flow of words and music, the waves crashing on Ferris Beach as I spun around and around because I couldn't take in enough of the air and sea gulls as they swooped and whined. Angela was energy, the eternal movement of the world, the blood in my veins and the wind in the bare winter branches that creaked and cried out in the night like tired ghosts in search of a home" (6–7). Also, when they first meet, Angela first touches and then kisses Kate's birthmark, a sign to Kate that Angela both acknowledges and accepts her vulnerability.

As Angela appears and reappears in the novel, Kate learns more about the reality of her cousin's life—failed marriages, violent relationships, financial irresponsibility, lack of dependability—but her first impression of Angela at Ferris Beach is so strong that she rejects the truth in favor of the illusion she has created, and perhaps Kate feels obligated to love her cousin's weaknesses in the same way that Angela has shown acceptance of Kate's birthmark. Although Angela's name seems ironic in terms of her behavior, in fact, Kate sees her as a sort of "guardian angel," someone "to look up to, someone [she] could imagine in a lofty protected part of the sky, who could . . . make sense of [Kate's] placement in the world" (66). But this, of course, is just another part of the fairy tale Kate has invented. In several ways McCorkle connects Angela to fairy tales in the novel, a signal that she is illusive, lacking substance, but it is not until the end of the novel, after Kate has watched several other role models fall short of her expectations, that Kate can accept Angela as the imperfect being she is.

A second surrogate mother for Kate is her friend Misty's mother, Mo Rhodes. When Mo and her family first move to Kate's neighborhood, Kate is drawn to her because of her eccentricities—she wears pink toenail polish and dangling earrings, paints her house electric blue, and turns her front yard into a Japanese rock garden. In the same way that Angela kisses Kate's birthmark when they first meet at Ferris Beach, both Mo and Misty comment on the mark at their first meeting. Kate's mother, on the other hand, wants Kate to ignore the mark, to pretend it does not exist, to be happy she does not have some worse defect, but what Kate wants is exactly what Angela, Mo, and Misty give her—honesty. She wants people to acknowledge her weaknesses and then accept her as she is.

Mo represents to Kate everything that her own mother is not. She is creative, bold, entertaining, and accepting. She wishes, as she wishes with Angela, that "Mo Rhodes would adopt" her (54), feeling envious of Misty's great luck in daughterhood. Eventually she learns the truth about Mo—that she is not the ideal mother and has been having an affair with a family friend, Gene Files, for years—and Kate is stunned but still resists the truth. Photographs again play an important role in this work by McCorkle, illustrating the contrast between appearance and reality of Mo as a mother. In one scene Kate is invited into the Rhodes home, where the family is preparing for a picture of two families who seem to be great friends. In time, the truth of this photo is revealed: it is a picture of two lovers and their unknowing spouses. As Kate encounters more and more tragedy in her life, she remembers photographs of happier times, but she realizes that photographs are merely frozen moments of time and are not always depictions of reality; she accepts that most pictures—which show seemingly happy moments—are not the truth. The "photos that win prizes" are those which show "moments of torture and pain, those moments when human faces . . . split to reveal the deepest, darkest fears" (112).

In keeping with McCorkle's trend in earlier books, holidays set the scene for tragedy, times when Kate's awareness about life and love is heightened. And so it is on Independence Day when Mo Rhodes (with her baby, Buddy) and Gene Files leave their families to run away together—leaving Kate feeling "vulnerable [and] exposed" (105). In the tense days that follow, Mo agrees to return home temporarily, but on the way home all three are killed in a car accident, leaving Kate feeling that Mo "took with her some knowledge of [Kate's] own life" (115). The car wreck seems a fitting end to Kate's shattered image of Mo as the perfect woman/mother. Later, when she admits that sometimes she feels "so homesick, only to discover that what [she] was missing was Mo" (208), she is not nostalgic for the flesh-and-blood Mo but rather the idea and ideal of Mo. She has lost not just a role model but her innocence as well.

The illicit love affair of Mo Rhodes and Gene Files is not the only time Kate encounters conflicts over sexuality. A third female role model for Kate is connected to her growing sexual feelings, fears, and questions. Perry Loomis is a beautiful girl in Kate's class at school, who—despite her popularity with the boys—is culturally and economically deprived. Kate admits that most girls despise Perry for her beauty and sexual attractiveness, but Kate idolizes her, connecting her feelings to those she has for Mo and Angela when she says, "I saw her in the same way I saw Angela, the way I had seen Mo, glittering and shining, rare like a jewel" (141). Kate's illusion of Perry's romantic life is destroyed when on Christmas Eve she becomes the unwilling witness to the gang rape of Perry by neighborhood boys. Stuck hiding in a tree and unable to help Perry, Kate suffers along with her, and when she tries to sleep that night, Kate sees "Perry's eyes wide and frightened, her face frozen in silent terror . . . those breasts that were the subject of all the adolescent boys' dreams of womanhood and sexiness, just those of a young girl, pale blue veins underlining pale white skin, breast bone as fragile as that of a chicken ripped and torn apart" (219). Kate is only beginning to become aware of her own sexuality, and this ordeal has strong formative implications. Contrary to her naive beliefs about love and sex, this experience teaches her that love and sex are not always connected and that beauty can be a curse as well as an advantage. Most important, Kate realizes her physical fragility as a female in a male world.

McCorkle connects two significant images to Kate's observation of the rape; first, she hangs a "fairy-tale moon" over the scene which contrasts violent reality with illusive romance, as well as associating the moon with femaleness. Second, the memory of Perry's fear triggers images of Mo's death—"the look of horror as she screamed out in that brief second, her hand reaching out for Buddy"—and Misty's grief—"clinging to the carport post and screaming for her mother to come back, her hair wild against the dark sky" (219). To Kate at this point, love of any kind seems destructive and injurious. Near the end of the novel, when Kate's mother discovers her in bed with her boyfriend Merle and Kate becomes convinced she must run away with Angela to Ferris Beach, Kate sees Angela's choices in life as valid. In her anger at her mother's violation of her private moment of peace, Kate thinks, "No wonder Angela left home; I envied her that freedom, the time she had run away and gotten married, the time she had said that the world could go to hell, she was doing as she pleased" (323).

The trip to Ferris Beach, though, proves to be the final conflict between illusion and reality and the final shattering of childhood fantasies that Kate has been harboring. At Angela's apartment in Ferris Beach, which McCorkle describes as seedy, dingy, and squalid, Kate finally confesses her dream of being Angela's child, and Angela reminds her that orphanhood is her story and not Kate's, telling her the truth about ideal mothers: "'We all want a fairy tale, Kitty,' she whispered. 'Nobody wants the truth. But sooner or later you learn that there are no fairy tales; there *is* no glamorous mother hidden on a faraway island, no prince on a white horse, no treasure chest full of jewels. . . . That's the real story and the truth is that I'm sorry that's the truth'" (330, 334). Reminiscent of the fairy-tale moon described several times earlier in the novel, this imagery marks the moment when Kate finally sees through her own illusions. Even her feelings about Ferris Beach change; early in the novel she describes it as a place with "huge Ferris wheels and strings of blinking lights, and cotton candy whipped and spun around a paper cone" (18), but after she grows through experience and tragedy, she sees the place in all its tawdriness, a place with bait-and-tackle shops, trailer parks, run-down apartments, and a pier.

Ferris Beach is a novel full of tragedy—not only about females but about males as well. Kate's father is an important figure in the novel and in Kate's life for many reasons. For female heroes, the father figure is important because he "first indicates to her what her identity in the patriarchal world will be,"[6] a role made even more important in the male-oriented culture of the South. Typically in earlier southern fiction, a female hero realizes her access to power is only through her father, and therefore she does not initially reject him as she rejects her mother. Unlike male heroes, who gain power by eventually supplanting the father, the female hero eventually accepts her subordinate position in the male world and becomes "feminized"—as in McCullers's *The Member of the Wedding* and *The Heart Is a Lonely Hunter* and Harper Lee's *To Kill a Mockingbird.* This pattern, however, has been altered by third-generation southern women writers such as McCorkle.

In *Ferris Beach* Kate's father, Fred, is a lovable man who teaches math at the community college. Ironically, his math background does not make him the logical and rational being in the family; instead, he is the stereotypical creative, eccentric southerner, a man who is a dreamer. He is the parent with whom Kate first identifies—perhaps because of his southern roots, perhaps because of his humor and his penchant to break the rules, perhaps even because she recognizes that her own mother is powerless as

a faux southerner and a woman. Part of the heroic journey, however, is coming to terms with the father's weaknesses as well as
the mother's. Understanding that she cannot depend upon her
father to shelter her from tragedy is one of the awakenings Kate
experiences in the course of the novel. This awareness is symbolized in a scene in which Kate and her father are feeding ducks at
a pond. Gulls flying overhead steal the bread from one of the
ducks that could not "get its long clumsy neck bent in the right
direction." As Fred continues trying to get pieces of bread to the
hungry bird, suddenly the duck "turned, beak open, and clamped
down on one of the gulls; there were shrill screams and feathers
spewing as the duck shook its stiff neck from side to side." Kate
screams and begs her father to "make them stop," but he is unable
to do anything to end the violence before the gull is dead. Fred
puts his arms around his daughter and says, "'Sorry you saw that.
. . . And I'm sorry I couldn't stop it all'" (278–79). Such unex-
plainable violence and tragedy exist in the world, he seems to be
saying, and ultimately, no one can protect us.

Kate comments that her parents "never looked like they
went together." In their wedding picture, Kate keeps expecting
"the real spouses to step in from the wings on either side" (3).
Her father is thin and her mother is large, and so Kate relates
them to the fairy-tale figures Jack Sprat and his wife. According to the nursery rhyme, Jack Sprat and his wife—despite their
physical differences—make a perfect couple because together
"they lick the platter clean." Kate, though, can only see their
differences, not how they complement each other. Judging her
parents' marriage on appearances alone is one of the mistakes
that leads Kate to her misconceptions about love in general.

Believing that her parents did not belong together because they look so different, Kate mistakenly assumes they cannot and do not love each other.

When Kate's father dies suddenly from a heart attack, she is overwhelmed with grief. Unlike much of the earlier southern fiction mentioned—which removes the mother from the equation altogether—McCorkle subtracts the father, leaving Kate to work through her differences with her mother. Kate, however, has never discussed love or sex with her mother, and her personal knowledge is limited to a relationship with Merle Hucks, the neighborhood boy with whom Kate discovers sexual longing and with whom she loses her virginity. This situation, too, turns tragic when, in their second and final sexual experience before Merle moves away, Kate's mother interrupts them in bed, screaming words of blame and shame. Kate's last thoughts during this scene are centered on her father, the one who had always been the peacemaker in the family. She remarks simply, "He was not there to settle this mess" (321).

At this point in the story, most of Kate's childhood illusions have been shattered: ideal love seems impossible, loss seems inevitable, and comfort seems out of the question. A sense of vulnerability and a lack of security have been growing throughout the course of the novel. Kate had always turned to her friend Misty for affirmation, but once Mo Rhodes leaves her family, Misty becomes cynical. Like Jo Spencer in *The Cheer Leader,* Kate feels unprotected and exposed—symbolized by the birthmark which everyone can see. She searches for answers to life's unanswerable questions; she believes that there is a "truth" to be known but that the ones who could have told her the "secret"—Mo and her father—are taken from her before they have the chance.

Part of her search—and Misty's—leads to religion, but McCorkle offers little in the traditional forms of religion that can give them comfort or answers. In fact, religion is handled satirically in *Ferris Beach* most of the time. A church retreat, which Kate and Misty attend, seems a parody of modern religion, juxtaposing traditional beliefs with modern culture to illustrate how ineffectual and absurd religion can seem in the contemporary world: "*Jesus Christ Superstar* wasn't good enough; these people were set on writing their own opera that weekend. The climax came when Jesus went up to the Woman at the Well and sang 'Hello, I Love You'; somehow it didn't seem to be what either Jesus or Jim Morrison had intended" (56). The young adults are given new names with religious meaning, but these are often transformed into something absurd; for example, Frankincense inevitably becomes Frankenstein, and Kate's name Agape is mispronounced "*agape.*" In an equally absurd scene during the Fulton Christmas Parade, the "high school drama students who were manning the float had *live* animals, and . . . Joseph had thrown down his walking stick and was wrestling a sheep who was butting the chicken wire that enclosed the flatbed trailer" (146). Finally, Kate describes the "modernization" she and her friend Misty give to church hymns: "Whenever my mother allowed me to sit with Misty in church, we played a game where we'd close our eyes, open the hymnal, and then read the two titles with an ending of 'in the bed,' such as 'Just As I Am *in the bed*' or 'How Great Thou Art *in the bed*'" (157). While these first appear as simply comic children's games, they subtly suggest that religion often seems unsuitable or out of place when juxtaposed with modern life— offering little or no comfort—and is more often cause for laughter.

The girls experiment with various approaches to answer-finding. Misty eventually adopts and clings to the belief of pre-destination, "the belief that her mother's life had no other course than the one taken" (120). While such a belief gives comfort to Misty, this explanation seems inadequate to Kate, who cannot "stop thinking about the prayers, flying upwards, crisscrossing like the airwaves, one request put on hold while another is answered" (120). Such arbitrary spiritual assistance seems unfair, and Kate is left with more questions than answers. Kate's beliefs lean toward the humanistic, having no specific answers but believing that in the large pattern of the universe there is meaning. Such a belief structure, however, offers little solace to Kate most days, leaving her with more feelings of vulnerability to chance and fate.

Many times in the novel, she voices her anxiety about the lack of guarantees in this life. The first time she has sex with Merle, she does so because of her fear of the future, fear of not knowing if life has a purpose, fear of her own mortality. She justifies her actions: "I was going to pretend that there was no day other than this one, no world beyond those trees; there was no future, no guarantee that I would turn sixteen, this was it" (281). The only other time Kate and Merle have sex is also ini-tiated by Kate's despair, this time because Merle's family is moving away. Kate states: "There were no guarantees that I'd see him again, no guarantees that my mother and Angela would make it home from the lawyer's office, no guarantees that I'd wake up tomorrow or that I'd ever turn seventeen or that there was any kind of life waiting for me. . . . I turned to him then, urgent and panicked, more sure than ever before that there were no guarantees" (318). This carpe diem philosophy is based on fear and the destruction of Kate's childhood illusions, and it does not serve her well.

If the novel ended on this note, it would be a bleak novel, indeed. But McCorkle has only broken down Kate's defenses and fractured her illusions in preparation for the real moment of understanding in her life, a moment which is tied to the acceptance of her mother. After losing the two strong male figures in her life—Merle and her father—and becoming disillusioned with her three female role models—Angela, Mo, and Perry—Kate has no one to turn to except her mother. But desperation and loneliness are not the keys to Kate's growth; instead she realizes that her mother, like the other figures in her life, is not what she had believed. After her father dies, Kate witnesses her mother's grief, and she is faced for the first time with a true picture of her mother as a woman who truly loved her husband. Kate finally asks the question for which she had always assumed a negative answer: "'You really did love him, didn't you?'" (342). Far from the romantic relationship Kate has imagined true love to be, her parents' love in the end proves to be the one which endures, and Kate is forced to reexamine her own definitions of love. Barriers of communication are not easy to overcome, however, and McCorkle does not force a happy ending. Kate comments: "My mother never mentioned that day to me, and though we often talked our way around it, it seemed I could never get close enough to tell her I was sorry I had ever wished her away. That I *was* my mother's daughter, and that for every time she had misjudged me, I had also misjudged her" (341). Kate's "orphanhood" has ended with the acceptance of her real mother.

Paralleling Kate's reconciliation with her mother is the relationship between Misty and her new stepmother, Sally Jean. Sally Jean's vulnerable spot is the inevitable comparison between herself and everyone's memory of Mo—a woman whose sin of abandonment is forgiven because of her tragic death. Taking another woman's place would be difficult enough, and it becomes even harder because Misty so fiercely resists Sally Jean's involvement in her family. Sally Jean plays an important role in this novel because her presence—while seeming to be relatively insignificant—carries symbolic weight. One of the major problems among characters in this novel is lack of communication. Characters speak to each other, but more than not, they only say part of what they mean for fear of exposing their own vulnerabilities or someone else's. McCorkle symbolizes this lack of communication with Sally Jean's speech, which is packed with malapropisms. Since malapropisms occur inadvertently and the speaker is never aware of her/his error, McCorkle suggests that people often do not communicate simply out of ignorance. In Sally Jean's case, she desperately wants to fit in with her new family and new community, but she initially lacks the ability to do so. She is blissfully ignorant of her errors, and her statements glitter with such comic gems as "her house was anesthetically pleasing" and "'Thomas has said that I can sodomize our yard'" (162, 242).

This miscommunication theme is furthered in the epitaph for Fred's grave that he had ordered years before. He had requested the lines by one of his favorite poets, Alfred Lord Tennyson: "Break, break, break, at the foot of thy crags, O Sea! But the tender grace of a day that is dead will never come back to me." Unfortunately, the man who chisels the verse "put *grave* instead of *grace* and *dad* instead of *day,*" sending a wrong, but equally meaningful and somewhat humorous, message: "But the tender grave of a dad . . . will never come back to me" (289). Kate understands her father's meaning, but her mother does not, and it leads her to question whether she understood the man at all. It also, however, leads to a confrontation between Kate and her mother which ultimately brings them together in their grief over the loss of Fred.

The rediscovery of her identity as daughter changes Kate's fatalistic outlook, and she realizes that although there are still "no guarantees," there are definitely "possibilities" and "second chances." Kate has grown to understand that everyone has a "birthmark," that spot of weakness the world attacks: Fred's "one blind spot" is Angela (292); for Merle, it is his background, a "trashy" family enveloped in poverty and social stigma. As a young girl, Misty is overweight, and even when she loses weight, that "pressure spot was still there" (201). Kate's mother is insecure about her husband's devotion to Angela, and when Angela comes to visit, Kate notices "a vulnerability" she sees at no other time (172). Second chances are available for nearly everyone, though. Even Merle, who leaves Fulton, finds "a new start, a second chance" in a town only thirty miles away (341). Ultimately it is not religion but a human being that provides Misty with her opportunity, her new stepmother, Sally Jean, who becomes "an answer to a prayer, a second chance" (343). And the women in Kate's family get another chance as well: "In a way my mother and I *were* getting that second chance. And maybe Angela was looking for her new chance; maybe she had already found it." As the book ends, Kate acknowledges that "a whole world of possibilities" is "spinning around her," perhaps a much more valuable existence than a world filled with guarantees (342–43).

In this novel McCorkle has done an excellent job in capturing the insecurities held by everyone, but especially by young girls, idealistic by nature but facing a world without the guarantee of happiness they have read about in fairy tales. The idealism of such stories which is fed to children is replaced in the novel with a better "food": the belief in people, in possibilities, and in self-direction.

CHAPTER SIX

Crash Diet: Stories

In 1992 McCorkle published *Crash Diet: Stories,* bringing together eleven stories that had been published in various forms in journals, magazines, or anthologies.[1] The stories all center around a different female protagonist who, during the course of the story, becomes aware that her life is far from being the fairy tale that she was "promised" as a small girl, that life is not working out the way she had planned, and that she must reinvent herself in order to survive and thrive. As McCorkle stated in an interview with Elinor Ann Walker, her protagonists are "women who in the midst of this ordinary, middle class life all of a sudden look up and it occurs to them that they are people too," finding themselves, as Walker perceptively observes, "not so much 'love-lorn' as 'love worn.'"[2] In addition, each character experiences a "sense of loss, something that cannot be recaptured," and so must find "a level of acceptance, or in some way [deal] with the void."[3]

Unlike many female characters found in traditional southern fiction, though, these women do not find solace in their families, churches, or communities; in fact, as Walker also notes, what makes their stories different from earlier stories about southern women is that "what usually sustains their female characters— some sense of family or community—is often the very thing that fails the women." Instead, each female character explores her newly dismantled life and decides to re-create her own space and identity in any way that she can. One way McCorkle's protagonists accomplish this is through their narrative voices. Using

first-person point of view in nine of the eleven stories is significant because the technique allows each woman to take control of
her own story, to "write one's own script," and "let narrative, not
network television and SlimFast commercials, shape" her life.[4]

Reviews of the book were generally very favorable, although
some stories were received more positively than others. The weakness identified most often is the "sameness of the narrative voice"
and the lack of plot—rather that some stories are "an extended
mood, not a story." These kinds of remarks have usually been
made by male reviewers who perhaps expect more traditional patterns of plot construction. McCorkle structures these stories in a
very "female" way, focusing on subtle development of character
and internal monologue rather than traditional exposition leading
to a climax. Overwhelmingly, though, critics have agreed that
when the stories work, McCorkle proves herself one of the best
new writers to enter the literary scene. Greg Johnson, writing for
The Georgia Review, for one, found *Crash Diet: Stories* an
"immensely entertaining and readable collection" that "offers an
engaging blend of humor and pathos."[5] And despite McCorkle's
own misgivings about writing short stories—she calls them her
"orphans"—she proves herself worthy of writing many more.

"Crash Diet"

McCorkle began writing the title story with only a voice and a situation in mind: Sandra Barkley's husband, Kenneth, leaves her
for a younger woman, Lydia. Sandra is similar to many of
McCorkle's women characters: feisty but basically low on self-
esteem, independent yet still needing the respect and love of a

good man, tough but only to a point—in this case, the "crash" that comes not when her husband leaves her, but when her energy derived from anger runs out. The story, which first appeared in *Cosmopolitan,* chronicles Sandra's process of working her way through the loss of her husband and the end of her marriage and is similar to the loss one would experience with a death of a loved one. First, she seems disbelieving, denying the situation. When Kenneth first admits he has been having an affair, rather than cry or fight, she starts "working on the mold that wedges in between those tiles in the shower stall" (3–4), and when he says he is leaving to move in with Lydia, she remarks with irony, "'Well, give her my best'" and "'Send me a postcard'" (2).

Because the story is told from Sandra's point of view, the reader is left wondering if Kenneth is worth suffering for. He is a man who challenges Sandra's gift for their fifth wedding anniversary, a microwave, with the words "'But this is a big investment'"—bigger, it seems, than the five years he has invested in his marriage, which he seems so ready to discard (3). Kenneth is a bartender at the local Holiday Inn and therefore finds it amusing to live in a subdivision where all the streets are named after liquor: Tequila Circle, Seagrams, Marnier Street, and so on. As with many of the male characters in *Crash Diet: Stories,* McCorkle makes Kenneth both pathetic and absurd. In fact, as Jack Butler from *The New York Times* notes, "there are no good men in these stories. There are not even any attractive men—and only one or two who show the faintest glimmer of anything resembling intelligence, sensitivity or loyalty."[6] Kenneth may represent the best of what is available, however, from the perspective of these women who expect to live happily ever after but face instead failure and loss. This is a theme McCorkle works in many of the stories in *Crash Diet: Stories*—that is, that young girls absorb from fairy tales the idea that each girl is a princess waiting for the handsome prince to arrive and carry her off to marital bliss—until reality exposes the hollowness and futility of such expectations.

McCorkle includes a great deal of humor in Sandra's next inevitable stage which follows denial: anger channeled into revenge. Sandra changes the title of Kenneth's car to her name and threatens to report it stolen to the police; she goes on a spending spree with Kenneth's credit card; she toilet papers Lydia's house while wearing her new black silk dress; she pampers herself with a day at a beauty spa. Most significant, though, is Sandra's weight loss. She blames the breakup of her marriage on the fact that she had gained weight in the five years since their wedding, even though when he decides to leave her she has lost thirty of the forty pounds already. When Kenneth leaves, her dieting becomes obsessive and unconscious, a focus for her anger and sadness. Her weight loss may even be an attempt to lose the literal weight of her husband while at the same time punishing herself for not being the ideal woman represented in women's magazines, billboards, and movies—convinced, perhaps, that it is her own flaws that have made her husband fall out of love with her.

The "diet" leads to the inevitable "crash," but she must crash before she can move on to the next stage: true healing and growth as a woman and an individual and the development of a clearer identity. When Sandra checks into the hospital because she has lost too much weight, she registers as "Lydia Barkley," illustrating her lack of understanding about who she will be once she is no longer Sandra Barkley—a sort of synthesis of her husband's name and the woman he claims to love more than Sandra. While in the hospital, she is fed both physically and emotionally. When the reader next sees Sandra, she is out of the hospital and clearly on the road to recovery, planning a dinner party for the people in her "new" life.

She is a different woman in many ways. When Kenneth stops by her house to ask Sandra to sign the divorce papers, she is wearing a black silk dress (appropriate attire for the party, in contrast to the last time she wore the dress, to toilet paper Lydia's house). The description of Sandra signing the papers indicates that she has tentatively begun her journey of self-growth: "I focused instead on signing my name, my real name, in my own handwriting, which if it was analyzed would be the script of a fat person. Some things you just can't shake; part of me will always be a fat person and part of Kenneth will always be gutter slime" (17). In this seemingly simple scene, McCorkle reveals several important ideas: First, Sandra is working on her identity, knowing and being the woman she is, not the woman she wishes she were. Second, Sandra realizes she will always have to manage her insecurities; her "fat self" will always be with her. Finally, Sandra has learned to live with opposing ideas, specifically that Kenneth is both bad and good, just like herself.

The guests at the dinner party represent Sandra's reconstructed life, which fuses people from her old life—her friend Paula, her mother, her beautician—with people from her new one—her therapist, the manager of Revco (where she spent so much of Kenneth's money). Other signs of growth are also apparent in Sandra: she has gained enough weight to have "love handles," and she is planning on writing Kenneth a check to help pay off his MasterCard bill. All is not perfect, though; McCorkle leaves problems and mysteries. Sandra still cannot relate to her mother, and Alan, her psychiatrist, is seeing Sandra on a personal basis—but to end the story otherwise would be too much like the fairy tales that misled Sandra in the first place. The last line of the story indicates a tempered hope: "You can do okay in this world if you can just find something worth holding on to" (19). This line suggests that Sandra must be enough of a "whole" person—that is, carry enough physical weight—to have love handles so that people who love her can grab on both physically and emotionally. On the other hand, Sandra confesses that she enjoys being thinner: "When you think about it, if your hipbones have been hidden for years and years, it's a real pleasure to have someone find them, grab hold, and hang on" (19).

Balance is the key, then. After feeling like the yo-yo with which she can do tricks, Sandra learns to balance both her physical and emotional selves, and like the narrators in *The Cheer Leader* and *Tending to Virginia,* McCorkle leaves the reader—and Sandra—with a stable but always evolving life, having thrown out the fairy-tale expectations and awaiting what will come next.

"Man Watcher"

Fairy tales again play an important role in McCorkle's second story, which originally appeared in *The Crescent Review.* "Man Watcher" is an extended monologue given by a woman who has become embittered by the failure of her first marriage and has therefore decided that true love and romance belong solely in stories told to children. Having failed to recognize love by using her heart, she has decided instead to use the scientific approach—cataloguing, analyzing, and dismissing one man after another when they fail to pass her "tests."

The narrator is a disillusioned Cinderella, named Lucinda and called Luci or Cinda. Her father has recently died, leaving her to deal with her "evil step-mother" and "self-centered step-sister" Lorraine. Like Cinderella, Luci's small feet cause jealousy in these other women, who have "big snowshoe-type feet" (22–23), and like many women, Luci was "desperately seeking once upon a time," an idealistic and unreliable approach, she feels now, to finding true love (29). She met her first husband at a Halloween party, and, taken in by his painted face, married him the next week—before discovering that she needed more time to get to know the man behind the "mask."

In response to this failure, Luci begins to catalogue men in the same way that birds are classified, noting their "natural habitats, diet, mating rituals" (21). By ignoring the emotional heart and focusing on the scientific head, Luci hopes to avoid another romantic catastrophe, but what she ends up doing is, in fact, finding a reason not to fall in love at all: "I passed [my time] by searching for the perfect male, dissecting specimen after specimen only to find his weaknesses and toss him aside" (31–32). By finding the flaws in every man she meets, she can justify never again offering her heart.

The result is a bitter woman who fears risk, fears having to depend on anyone else for happiness, fears having to make any compromises for love. This is a characteristic which seems to have developed early in Luci's life, perhaps as a result of first her mother's and then her father's deaths, leaving her an orphan just like Cinderella. As a child she convinced herself that she needed no one else. She claims that preparing to go to "Girl Scout camp gave me my first taste of self-sufficiency," by buying miniature sizes of toiletry items, which "represent independence." At camp she continued to grow in independence: "For that week . . . I was able to pull myself inward, to turn and flip until I was as compact as one of those little plastic rain bonnets. It was the key to survival. . . . It was my spirit that I had found. Of course I lost it the very next week once I was back home and doing as I pleased when I pleased, but I couldn't forget the freedom, the power my little sack of *essentials* had brought me" (26). She has decided that shampoo, toothpaste, and such are essential, but love is not.

Having decided that love makes her too vulnerable, Luci protects herself by remaining unattached. She fears losing her independence as a woman, claiming, "'I would never have a man of the church, and I would never have a man of the military. I don't want anybody telling me what to do or inspecting me'" (27). Both the military and the traditional church are patriarchies that traditionally require the subservience of women, thus her statement to avoid both. It is ironic, however, that she has reacted to this fear by doing the same thing: "inspecting" the opposite sex, looking for flaws. In fact, she has simply reversed the patriarchy—casting herself in the role of hunter and males in the role of prey.

Many authors have used birds to symbolize women. Writers such as Kate Chopin, Eudora Welty, Susan Glaspell, and Bobbie Ann Mason, as well as others too numerous to mention, have used bird imagery to represent the fragility, the beauty, and the imprisonment and restriction of women, often suggesting that women must be freed from their cages and allowed to stretch their wings and fly,[7] but McCorkle has reversed this structure in "Man Watcher." The final paragraph illustrates the extent of Luci's "bird-watcher" role: "I guess in a way I'm waiting for the rarest breed of all, my sights set so high I have to squint to keep the sky in focus. I concentrate on migration habits. I keep in mind that owls fly silently at night. Some people (like Lorraine) might say I'm on a snipe hunt. But, call me an optimist. I'm sitting here in a pile of ashes, waiting for the phoenix to take shape and rise" (36). Is this an improvement? Is reversing the order of life from patriarchy to matriarchy the answer? Of course not, but this is something that Luci has not yet learned. Her idealism that she, too, can rise from the ashes like the phoenix leaves the reader hopeful, but Luci is far from ready for that.

Just as Sandra in "Crash Diet" must learn the importance of balance, Luci will need to balance her head and heart in order to succeed in a relationship. As the story ends, she is still swinging wildly from one extreme to another—from absolute dreamer to cynical realist. Neither extreme will work, but only the reader sees this. McCorkle gives some indication that there is hope for Luci, who does say at one point that "there is something about the large and small of the world, the connections and movement between the two that keeps me in balance" (35), but she has not yet begun to apply this principle in her life. "Happily ever after" is still just a dream.

"Gold Mine"

McCorkle's third story, originally published in *The Greensboro Review,* portrays a married couple who wed soon after high school, inherited a motel on Highway 30 in South Carolina, and worked it into a profit-making enterprise until I-95 opened, which stole away all the traffic and business. McCorkle parallels the decline of the motel with the decay of Ruthie and Jim's marriage, as the American Dream for the pursuit of both wealth and happiness appears to be dying simultaneously.

McCorkle uses death imagery throughout the story, such as the highway "died" a "quick tragic death," leaving a "ghost town of pastel-painted motor lodges" with "no resurrection in sight" (37, 46, 45)—the social commentary being that the South and its personal touches, its regional flair, its separate identity, is being swallowed up in an onslaught of the American homogeneity of Wal-Marts, Taco Bells, and Holiday Inns. Ruthie has decorated each room in their motel differently, giving each a distinct atmosphere such as "Tahitian Treat," "Forest Foliage," and "Lavender Lace." The new American travelers, however, are no longer looking for charm or character; they want to feel at home wherever they go, and that means staying in rooms that could be in any hotel in any city or town in America.

Another parallel is evident here, as well, for the marriage falls victim to Jim's attraction to a younger woman, Barbara, whom he meets at a local community college. She is an instructor there and is bright, attractive, and not worn down by children, bills, or years. As Ruthie acknowledges, "Barbara is like I-95. She is fast and lively and young, and Ruthie is 301, miles of tread stains and no longer the place to go" (55). It seems that the easy consumerist philosophy—using things until they no longer please us or until they seem used and then replacing them with a new model quickly and easily rather than fixing up the old—has translated to people and marriages as well. Is the American Dream of prosperity and a good family life—their "gold mine"—still something people believe they must work for, or is it something people expect to be given with little or no effort?

Necessary to the American Dream, McCorkle suggests, is the sanctity of the family unit, and she symbolizes this fittingly with signs often seen in small motels alongside roads such as Highway 301. When Ruthie and Jim are happily married and their motel is filled with passing travelers, they joyfully place the "No Vacancy" sign out together each night. But as the highway and marriage suffer with the passing of time, the "Vacancy" sign becomes rusted in place, a vacancy easily filled by another woman. Ruthie and Jim's son Rodney, in his anger and frustration, stands outside and hurls pebbles into a parking lot: "his goal is to hit the NO TRESPASS-ING sign" (38), an action that is too late, it seems, since Barbara has already trespassed into their lives and family. In the motel office, the auto calendar is turned to a page saying "MAY DAY" (53). If only every occurrence in life were marked so clearly; Ruthie failed to see her husband slipping away from her, and she wishes she could have asked a psychiatrist who once stayed with them, "What are the signs of a husband about to leave?" (48).

The dreams and illusions people have of a perfect life—illusions which are usually replaced with the reality of hard work and a mixture of pain and joy—play a major role in this story. Like many young couples, Ruthie and Jim dream and plan their lives together, but when things get bumpy, they seem to lack the staying power to make changes and rechart their future. Even after Jim leaves Ruthie for Barbara, she imagines the past with Jim romantically, as "always sunset and there's always a breeze. . . . It's always one of those days when her hair falls smooth as silk, glistening with gold highlights that show off her tan; and her legs are long and lean, graceful with every step, her stomach flat as she stands with her hands on her hips, white gauzy dress swirling around her," in spite of the fact that she knows in reality about humidity, pregnancy, and the fact that she has "never in her life owned a white gauzy dress" (39).

Ruthie's favorite room in the motel is called "Blue Moon," playing upon McCorkle's often-used symbol of illusion. During long, hot afternoons, Ruthie would take her baby, Rodney, there and rest, staring up "at the print she had hung of a big crescent moon over the sea" (42–43). The moon appears several more times in this story as a symbol for hope and for the necessity of having dreams, no matter how far the dreamer falls short. When Jim returns to Ruthie one night, asking for forgiveness, his headlights are "round white lights like moons," and Ruth wonders and hopes that "he's come home" (57). And finally, when Jim does stay home, Ruthie looks at her daughter playing in the pool, reaching toward the "round hazy lights, her small hand reaching for the moon" (62).

Without completely dismissing the possibility that the American Dream can come true, McCorkle suggests that achieving such a dream will take work and hope, in a sort of Thoreauvian balance between building that castle in the sky, but remembering to build a solid foundation under it.

"First Union Blues"

The title of this story (first published in *Southern Magazine*) at first seems fairly obvious: the narrator, Maureen Dummer, is a teller at the First Union Bank, and her story is certainly one worth singing the blues about. She is young, uneducated, apparently in credit card debt, and the single mother of one daughter. The right man never seems to come along, and her future appears to consist of handling other people's money, living vicariously through the rich patrons of the bank, and scratching her way through life living in a rented condominium. In fact, though, McCorkle's title more accurately describes something else: Maureen's monologue is really a lament over the mistakes of the "first union" in her life that mattered—Larry Cross, the father of her daughter Larrette and the "bad boy" she could not corral.

No matter how much Maureen tells the reader, it becomes harder and harder to accept that she believes what she is saying. The narrative reads as if she is trying to convince herself of her success, her smart thinking, her upward movement. She remarks many times, for example, that she is "not stupid"—in spite of her last name—yet clearly she has made and continues to make stupid decisions. She also claims, "'I live by my instincts,'" yet it appears that her instincts are generally bad. Her instincts tell her that she left her Mr. Coffee on, and so she drives home at lunch only to find she turned it off (64). She started dating Larry Cross "instinctively," but later, when he has bought himself a surfboard and disappeared, she states that her instincts told her that the relationship with him "wouldn't work" (67). In short, Maureen's instincts have always led her in the wrong direction.

Another trait Maureen boasts of having is "perspective." She believes that life has taught her "lessons" that she has the obligation to share with friends (and the reader). Her vision, however, is clouded and unreliable. She admits that she likes "that word—perspective" because it can "make something sound a lot more important than it is" (67), and although her retrospective sight is fairly clear—she wishes that she could take her past and "spread it all out on a piece of paper and take some Wite-out to it"—she has difficulty seeing that her reaction to her past mistakes has been the swinging of the pendulum from one extreme to another—and that she is not making better decisions, only different ones.

Specifically, Maureen has traded a relationship with Larry based on lust, good looks, and sex appeal for one with Earl Taylor, simply because Earl is as different from Larry as possible: "When I think of Earl, I think khaki and oxford cloth. When I think of Larry Cross, I think Levi's and loud Hawaiian shirts, and loud-colored swim trunks and gym shorts. Flashy—Larry Cross is flashy with the money he doesn't have and that little Spitfire convertible in bright orange that I was forever needing to jump with my VW Bug. Earl Taylor drives a Mazda, a nice, neat, plain, navy Mazda that he vacuums on a regular basis. . . . Night and day. That's what Larry Cross and Earl Taylor are" (74). Earl is not the man made in heaven, however, no matter how much Maureen would like to believe he is. McCorkle hints at his obsessive neatness when Maureen comments, "He took the shoes right off of my feet and cleaned up the bottom of them for me" (74). Whereas Larry made both the bed and Maureen "creak and groan," Earl can "get in and out of a bed and you don't even know he's been there," and he could not make the bedsprings "squeak if he did a somersault with bricks tied around his neck" (73, 82). But Maureen's heart has been trampled on, and she is willing to make this trade to get stability in her life. Her constant fears of a fire starting in her house—as her cousin Eleanore says, "'Mr. Coffee, iron, oven, it's always something'"—mirrors her fears of letting a fire start in her heart. Larry was pure fire, and Earl is definitely safe and cold.

Unfortunately, Maureen's new perspective will not serve her forever, but she will most likely keep up the facade as long as possible. When she wishes that Larry were somewhere, missing her and realizing what a fool he was for letting her go, she says, "Right now I can believe in that lie and keep it all in perspective" (86), a statement that can apply to many aspects of her life. In time, McCorkle suggests, Maureen will realize her feelings for Earl are just a reaction to her loss of Larry; when she breaks a regular Monday night date with Earl and he complains that "it's Monday" and "'Cagney and Lacy'" comes on, she shows early signs of realization and growth: "He states all that as a fact and I realize that all Earl has ever done to me is state facts. A fact is just a base, a foot in the door, to perspectives and instincts" (84). In this statement Maureen shows a glimmer of understanding that Earl cannot give her emotionally what she needs, but her words also refer to an earlier remark that being a teller is just "a foot in the door" to bigger things (64). McCorkle leaves the reader with hope that Maureen will eventually see the need to find a balance between the boring good boy and the exciting bad boy, between financial stability and working in a job she feels passionate about. She realizes—tentatively—that even though Earl told her he loved her, "love" is a word that is "used and misused and abused," and that simply using the word "isn't good enough" (81–82).

Maureen is a woman in the middle of an identity crisis, symbolized by the fact that she hates her name and considers marrying men based on a last name she "could probably live with" (70). She and Eleanore also dress in disguise so they will not be recognized as they drive by Eleanore's married lover's home to watch him or visit the grocery store when Maureen is supposed to be home sick from work. So for now, both Maureen and Eleanore are "Dummers," but McCorkle gives the reader adequate hope that they will eventually learn enough from life's lessons to gain real perspective.

"Departures"

McCorkle describes "Departures" as a "major turning point" in her writing. Critics seem to agree that this is one of the best stories in this collection. Greg Johnson, in *The Georgia Review,* writes that the story is "fully and compassionately imagined" and "has the force of a miniature novel."[8] McCorkle's voice, too, is new in "Departures." Whereas the first four stories have all centered around women of ages relatively close to McCorkle's own, the voice in the fifth story is that of an older woman. Perhaps the most poignant story in this collection, "Departures" is a narrative which explores the grieving of a widow of three years who spends her time visiting public places such as shopping malls and especially airports as she attempts to overcome her personal loss and loneliness by connecting with strangers who ask nothing of her in return. Anna Craven goes to "loud public places to absorb the emotions" (97), and "real or not, she wanted to be a part of something that was of her own design. She had to get out, go places, watch people" (106).

Anna's own children do not understand her. They have decided she is old and helpless and beyond having needs of her own, especially sexual needs, but McCorkle portrays a woman who has not withered with age or motherhood or widowhood, a woman who remembers what it is to have a good sexual relationship, even though it would shock her children to know that. Her memories of her husband are filled with thoughts of lovemaking, the conceptions of her children, romantic nights at the beach, and although she admits "she is convinced she can live with just about anything[,] it's what she can't live without that poses a problem" (100). As Anna points out, divorcées are expected to go out and have a good time drinking and dancing, but widows are "supposed to drink coffee and play mah-jongg" (88).

This is not the only truth Anna wishes she could tell her children, for she has realized a great deal since the death of her husband, Walter. When she and Walter were much younger, they would stay in a beach house for a week each summer, and while they are there, they notice an older couple in a nearby house who "became a joke for them." As in Hitchcock's movie *Rear Window,* they become voyeurs, creating personalities and lives for these people, calling them "the Vanderbilts." One night they follow the couple and are disappointed to find out that they, too, live ordinary lives. This couple is an older version of Anna and Walter, but at the time, Anna and Walter only recognize this subconsciously. One year, "Mrs. Vanderbilt" comes to the beach by herself, and Anna and Walter learn her husband has died. It is a moment of uneasy realization for them about such possibilities in their own future. Years later, as a widow, Anna wishes she had learned more from the experience. If she could go back in time, she would "cross the street and go stand by Mrs. Vanderbilt on the deck. She would take notes on loneliness (is it really possible to live with it?) and then rush back to her own bed to find Walter there, her love reaffirmed with his every breath" (114).

Throughout the narrative Anna's frequent trips to the airport reflect her impulse to share her knowledge with others, to pass on "the message: life is fragile, so very fragile" (112). When she and Walter were young, tragedy was only something that happened to others; they believed it "came to them from beyond the boundaries and frames of their everyday lives," but after Walter's heart attack and death, she understands that tragedy "came from within, a heart that had never threatened anything except too much love, a fragile, easily broken organ" (102). Anna knows concretely how love makes people vulnerable.

McCorkle weaves the theme of love and the inevitable loss of love throughout this story with parallel scenes. Anna witnesses people in malls and airports taking their lives and loves for granted, never realizing how easily it can all be lost. There is the small drama of a lost child finding its mother, a man with flowers waiting for his girlfriend to arrive, a couple kissing good-bye. When reality intrudes with superficial and self-absorbed personalities, Anna reconstructs the situations in her mind until they end happily; for example, when Anna hears a young girl at the airport complain that she has to spend a weekend with her father every three months, Anna knows by her next visit she "will have constructed a setting for this girl where she will be happily reunited with her father. The father and girl will ask in amazement why they didn't see years ago how silly their problems were" (113). Because she cannot reconstruct her own life, she reinvents the lives of strangers until it gives her peace.

Walter's last words to Anna, which she repeats several times in the story, were a breezy "'See you tonight, honey'" (112) spoken on the phone long distance from the West Coast. Of course she did not realize at the time that these were his last words—his "departure." In a parallel scene, the final paragraph of the story shows a young woman in an airport: "'See you tomorrow night,' she calls and blows a kiss to the tall dark-haired man stepping into the boarding tunnel. He lifts a hand and is gone" (114). Over and over again, Anna sees others saying good-bye, reminding her of Walter's and her own too-easily offered farewells to each other. Perhaps her trips to the airport are an attempt to relive that moment and say something more meaningful, and perhaps she wants to warn others that each departure may be the last one, that life is too fragile to waste a moment.

"Comparison Shopping"

McCorkle returns to first-person narration with a story about Norlina in "Comparison Shopping," first published in *The Southern Review*. In college, Norlina is the brooding, literary type who wears "thick ugly glasses" and spends her time writing feminist articles for an underground newspaper called ♀. Her roommate, Sue, in contrast, is beauty queen and sorority girl, "the perfect example of what [her] newspaper was trying to destroy: she was coy and superficial and wore makeup every day of the week" (117). Subconsciously, however, Norlina is desperate to fit in, and the story reveals the lengths some people will go to be accepted.

The story picks up several years after college, recently after Norlina has broken off a relationship with a naturalist, Byron, a relationship that, at the time she met him, seemed as if it would be her only romantic option. Together they "lived in a pup tent in the National Park" where they protected bears and trees and resisted the materialism of modern living. Byron's character may be a bit extreme, but McCorkle's depiction of him highlights her keen sense of humor. Byron marries the two of them himself, and instead of rings, they exchange "natural artifacts" (123), and he would "periodically take a vow of silence out of respect for the trees" (127). As desperate as Norlina is to be loved, even she cannot live with Byron for more than seven years. Eventually, she returns to the city, but she uses Byron as a measuring stick for all the other men she meets. Every time she sees a fault in her current date, she "comparison shops," contrasting him to Byron and therefore finding her date ultimately superior, based on such simple facts as nothing had "set up housekeeping" on his head (130).

As part of Norlina's quest for normalcy, she moves into a house in Sue's uniform subdivision, Windhaven Estates, where conformity reigns: people "all do the same things. Like if one person hangs out a flag just for the hell of it on some nondescript day, then by noon, all the flags are flying" (116). Fitting in with her new friends is very important to Norlina. She admits these new people "aren't the smartest on the planet," but "they are certainly more normal than Byron, and most importantly, they accept me as one of them" (127). Like many of the protagonists in *Crash Diet: Stories,* Norlina has simply exchanged one extreme for the other, and what she needs to find is middle ground. Still feeling like the unattractive coed who wants to be accepted by the popular crowd, Norlina makes the mistake of settling for "better than before" because she does not know if there will be an "even better" up ahead. Her narration is strewn with phrases such as "I could *still* maintain that life *could* be worse" (130) and "He's no dream man, but it's a lot better than being with Byron" (127). Eventually, though, when her friends humiliate her by making her the butt of their jokes on an inane nationally broadcast game show, she realizes that she has been selling herself short just to belong.

In retrospect, Norlina sees that she should have known earlier that exchanging one extremely bad situation for another is not an improvement. She admits that "it's sad sometimes how life is distorted by comparisons: good-better-best, when really you were never up to *good* at all" (129). In her dreams she envisions the perfect life with the perfect man and verbalizes what she will eventually come to understand consciously—the need for balance: "We are incognito; we fit into society but we do not live by it" (129). In the end she finds that she cannot live a life of complete individualism (like Byron) or complete conformity (like Sue). She knows that she must find her own identity separate from others, even if it means being alone and lonely. Norlina may not know exactly who she is yet or what she wants from life, but as she notes in the final paragraph, she does have a "firm list of what I *don't* want" (138). Having tried both extremes, she is looking for herself somewhere in the middle.

"Migration of the Love Bugs"

In "Migration of the Love Bugs" McCorkle again uses the voice of an older woman, Alice. Alice and her recently retired husband, Frank, have moved from their rent-controlled apartment in Boston to a trailer in Florida, and the two are having different reactions to this drastic change in their lives. Frank finally feels free in Florida. His career in Boston as a concrete worker—building "house foundations and driveways, sidewalks that will remain until the New England winters crack them" (139)—has left him with a craving for mobility. Whereas his work kept things from "budg[ing] an inch," he wants the ability to "'move at a moment's notice'" (148, 140), hence the migration to Florida and the mobile home.

Alice believes part of Frank's need for mobility is based on his fear of dying. She remembers years before, when their son Carl's cat grew old, Frank waited until his son and wife were out of the apartment and then "took the cat away so [no one] would have to see it die" (146). Moving to Florida may be Frank's way of removing himself from his home as he approaches old age and death. Alice comments, "I suppose he thought when one of us died the other could simply move away from the grief. His plan of action was as simple as taking a dying house cat from its home" (152). She knows Frank's first instinct is "to run" and his running is not so much "running *to* this new place as much as . . . running *away*" from the old one—a place where he was growing old and feeling useless (152). Alice resists old age in a different way: she does not "like change and never [has]" (141). She sees Frank's "Exodus" to "the Promised Land" of Florida instead as "Armageddon" (140, 141). Whereas Frank sees their old life as immobile and therefore stagnant, Alice equates their home with its "frozen" rent as "safe and stable" (145). For Alice, forty years of living and forty years of memories have been erased as easily as the painters put on "a fresh coat of paint that would hide all traces" of them (147).

CRASH DIET: STORIES

McCorkle's most prominent image in this story is the love bugs mentioned in the title. Alice draws many parallels between her life with Frank and these insects who are "chronically on the move" and who have only four stages in life: "hatch, have intercourse, produce, and die" (142). Like the bugs with their exoskeletal shells, Alice and Frank live in "a tin can" (139). Their destination is "always south," but when they get there, Alice is sure that the bugs will find it—as she finds Florida—"nothing like what they expected" (142, 145). The bugs have only one chance to reproduce, as did Frank and Alice, who tried for years before finally conceiving their son, Carl. They, too, are "looking for a place to . . . die" (144), and Alice wonders why they do not stop and "just stay put" (151). And finally, Alice feels so miserable and out of place in Florida that she says, "I might fly out and fling myself into the grille of a car" (150). Clearly, Alice and Frank are reacting to old age and impending death in different ways. As in the case of the love bugs, Alice and Frank's creation of an heir (and in turn, the recent birth of their grandson Joseph) has moved them into the final stage of their lives, closer to inevitable death. When Alice concludes that if the "bugs *knew* what was going to happen, they'd choose a celibate life and potential longevity" (144-5), she is actually wondering if her own demise could have been staved off without the younger generations chasing her into old age.

In the end Alice is the more philosophical and realistic of the two. She knows that life is short for both bugs and humans, and like Anna in "Departures," Alice wishes she could communicate that message to her son and his wife, that life is brief and fragile and must be appreciated fully at every stage. Unlike Frank, Alice knows "there is no Promised Land" and the only thing that truly matters is "the journey itself and all we left behind" (154). While Frank believes it is his job to "make the end easier for whoever is left behind"—perhaps by moving his wife away from the home filled with reminders of the past—Alice faces the future honestly, knowing that soon one of them, like the love bugs, "must take flight" (155).

"Waiting for Hard Times to End"

"Waiting for Hard Times to End" first appeared in *The Southern Review,* and, generally, reviewers have agreed that it is one of the most well-crafted stories in this collection. McCorkle's narrator is Saralyn (nicknamed Bunny by her older sister, Rhonda), a shy teenager who lives vicariously through the postcards she receives from her runaway sister, Rhonda. The relationship between the sisters is reminiscent of Kate and Angela in *Ferris Beach.* Just as Kate presumes with Angela, Bunny imagines Rhonda's life to be glamorous and romantic, when in reality Rhonda is much misused and abused by a litany of men who love and then leave her. Rhonda's ending is more tragic than Angela's, though: she is found murdered in a motel, shot, fittingly, "in the heart" (174).

Rhonda only writes to Bunny when times are good: when she is employed, in love, happy. The gaps in her postcards come during hard times, and Bunny is left to wait for the "hard times to end" with a new postcard announcing "WHEW" followed by an explanation filled with warnings against men and love. Her hard times—which include being robbed, abandoned, arrested and strip-searched, involved with a married man, and unemployed—are severe and tragic, but Bunny refuses to see Rhonda's life as anything but romantic and exciting: "I see Rhonda and a handsome man riding the Ferris wheel, while I stand on the ground and look up at them, a huge teddy bear in my arms that a boy like Rudy has won for me over at the shooting range" (169–70). Like Kate in *Ferris Beach,* Bunny must have her romantic illusions shattered before she can grow into a mature young woman. As long as Bunny believes Rhonda's love advice, she will be unable to move forward. Rhonda's postcards are filled with bad depictions of and warnings about men such as "they love you when they can get something. In your pants and in your wallet," and "They will use you to get what they want" (172, 173). Taking Rhonda's advice never works for Bunny, but she refuses to believe it is Rhonda's fault, instead blaming herself for her failures.

As long as Rhonda is alive, Bunny is unable to live her own life. Her worries over Rhonda seem parental in nature, and they affect her relationships with others. She was, for example, "so worried at the sophomore dance" that she spends the evening just sitting at her table (168), and she skips school during one of Rhonda's "hard times" because she is waiting for the mail to be delivered each day. She finds it difficult to make friends her own age, and because of Rhonda's warnings, she cannot relate to her family. Until Rhonda's death, Bunny finds it impossible to separate her own identity from Rhonda's. She only knows how to measure life by the yardstick of Rhonda's postcards. When the postcards stop because Rhonda is murdered, Bunny flounders, unable to make decisions without hearing Rhonda's postcard voice telling her what to do. When her mother calls her "Saralyn," she remarks, "I wanted to be called Bunny so bad I thought I'd die" (174), indicating her continuing desire to be Rhonda's little sister, shy and protected.

Forced into developing her separated identity after Rhonda is murdered, Bunny finally does ask others to call her Saralyn because, she says, "That's my real name" (176). Renaming herself as herself instead of Rhonda's sister is the first step in the creation of a separate self. Another indication of maturity is her recognition of the contrast between her vision of Rhonda's life suggested by the postcards and the reality of that life: "Sometimes I think I'd just rather stay right here and get the pictures of all those places, the lights and the bridges. And then all of a sudden I will see the other picture, the real picture that never did and never will be on a postcard, that motel room that night" (176).

Tragedy is what brings Bunny/Saralyn to a new awakening, a hard lesson to learn, but one that will shape her as a grown woman. As Jack Butler points out in his review in *The New York Times Book Review,* Bunny's salvation—like other protagonists in *Crash Diet: Stories*—"lies in plowing *through;* the separation and loneliness that beats them down may be what finally frees them from their narrow lives. In their suffering, they have a chance to escape the habits and assumptions that trap the people around them."[9]

"Words Gone Bad"

First published in *New Virginia Review,* this story is perhaps McCorkle's furthest stretch creatively in *Crash Diet: Stories.* The

CRASH DIET: STORIES

narrative voice is that of an elderly black woman, custodian in a foreign-language building at a university. Mary is a woman who is both tough and vulnerable, looking for significance in her life and a connection to others around her. Although never married, Mary raised six children, and her independence and determination have created a woman who expects help from no one. In her younger days she was "wild," and she socialized with other women who could "drink like mad," yet when the sun came up the next morning, she was always "among the standing." She prides herself in her strength: "I have never in my life had to be carried in no way" (179). This extends even to her relationship with God, a subject she and her coworker, Bennie, debate. Whereas Bennie believes in turning the other cheek, in seeking peace, and in believing the best about others, Mary believes that if there is peace, "'it ain't on this earth'" (181). For her, the "'price is too high'" to trust one's fate to God (180). She prefers not to be indebted even to God; she remarks, "I owe nobody nothing and Jesus himself would be ashamed to turn on me with a look of disgust" (195).

Despite her lack of education, Mary is perhaps McCorkle's most philosophical narrator in this collection. She has lived through the Civil Rights era, has seen the effects of both Malcolm X and Martin Luther King Jr., and she begins her narrative with the words "I don't believe in nonviolence" (177). Passivity, in her life, has gotten her nowhere. Speaking about her status as a black woman, she believes there was never "good weather for a woman like me" (182). She must take what she wants rather than wait for the world to decide to give it to her. This attitude sets up an interesting one-sided discussion of "words" and the meaning—or lack thereof—they have for a woman such as Mary. Appropriately, Mary works in a building where foreign languages are taught, and the words she hears from students in English or any other language are equally meaningless. While the students believe and act as though they are superior to Mary—using "fromage" when they just mean cheese, "spouting from a textbook, some fancy long-winded words," and using politically correct terms such as "African-American"—Mary knows their words are just "words and words and more words in their dusty slanted lines of white and yellow, erasers filled with words gone old or bad or both, used up day before yesterday and some not even in English" (183). Only their actions speak the truth: they leave their messes for her to clean up, they write their obscene words on bathroom walls, and they question her ability to pay bills simply because of her sex and color. They know, Mary believes, "'just enough . . . to put bad ideas into action'" (189).

Action is the key idea to Mary. During the Civil Rights Movement she "felt uplifted by the *ideas* and *beliefs* behind it all" (178), but things have not changed much in practice. She knows that writing the words "Give peace a chance" on a wall will inevitably be followed by someone writing "*fuck you* beneath it" (182). To mean something, words have to be backed up by actions. For Mary, "peaceful is what you feel *after* you've acted. . . . Peaceful is reserved for after the action, after you've done what you had to do" (185). For example, she likes to hear "African-American" used to describe her people, in the same way her great-grandmother "liked hearing *emancipation*," but more important than the word is the action showing the respect that goes along with the word: words, as she well knows, "can get washed off and thrown away" (187), for she has been the one to erase their words on the walls.

Bennie, Mary's newly retired coworker, often gets lost when Mary is philosophizing, perhaps because he naively wants to believe that people are generally good. As Mary tells him, though, "'Dirty can stay dirty without anybody's help but clean can't stay clean'" (191). A simple janitor metaphor, and yet it says a great deal. Mary knows that if she and others in her position simply sit back and wait, things will only get dirtier for them. To make something clean and better takes effort—action.

"Words Gone Bad" is a complicated short story, and it contains many rich ideas to explore. Like McCorkle's other narrators, Mary finds herself in a position where she can either give up and accept less in life or continue to struggle, trying to make a better world for herself as well as for her children.

"Sleeping Beauty, Revised"

Continuing the fairy-tale imagery found in some of the early stories in *Crash Diet: Stories,* McCorkle has written a revision for her "princess" in this story. Instead of waking up to the handsome prince who has come to take her away to her happy new life, McCorkle's nameless narrator wakes up to find herself divorced, a single mother of young Jeffrey, and the newest member of the dating scene. What follows could be subtitled "Plan B for the Princess," as she tries to figure out how to move forward in her life with her newfound cynicism and feminism. As Sandra Gilbert and Susan Gubar have so perceptively pointed out, the future of a fairy-tale princess is bleak from any perspective. At some point she will be replaced by her daughter, the new "fairest of them all," and become either the dead mother or the evil living avatar.[10]

In contrast to the narrator's situation, McCorkle includes two young women, a baby sitter and a waitress, who are premarriage and therefore still maintain their illusions of the handsome prince, the romantic marriage, and the happily-ever-after. The engaged baby sitter has chosen "Eternal by Lenox" as her fine-china pattern and misses the irony in the narrator's admission that she had chosen "Solitaire," and McCorkle describes the baby sitter's demeanor with words such as "dreamy" and "hypnotic" to suggest her unrealistic marital expectations (197–98). The waitress, named Betsy, serves the narrator and her blind date, Phil (and young Jeffrey), and by the end of the evening is surreptitiously exchanging telephone numbers with Phil. Both Phil and Betsy—neither of whom has been married—are described in fairy-tale terms because of their still-romantic ideas about happy endings: "He looks like he's in a trance, like the Prince when Cinderella enters the ballroom, the Prince when he finds Snow White in her glass coffin, the *Prince* when he makes his way to Sleeping Beauty's bedside" (208). His behavior, however, changes this image for the narrator, and he becomes a "picture ripped from a storybook—a two-dimensional prince," one that the narrator knows lacks the depth to understand her. Betsy, like Phil, is "still waiting to begin, waiting to choose her patterns. There's no slate to wipe clean" (212).

Having experienced real pain and loss, the narrator begins to look at fairy tales in a different way. Instead of focusing on the happiness and heroism inherent in such stories, she begins to notice the darker side that many people ignore—or try to modernize into politically correct tales. No longer "eligible" to play the princess role, she is assigned by her son, Jeffrey, "the sinister roles: witches and ogres and evil stepmothers" (199). When Phil comments that the original stories were horrible and violent, she replies, "'There are bad things that happen all over; why should fairy tales be excluded?'" (203).

Jeffrey, it seems, is suffering from his own feelings of abandonment, and his aunt Lenora has suggested that playing "these *violent* games" is his response to the divorce (199). His feelings in some ways parallel the narrator's. Pushed too soon into the role of hero for his mother, Jeffrey spends his days pretending to kill giants and spear crocodiles. In the restaurant he has a sudden awakening that "the fish that swim around in aquariums or talk, like in *The Little Mermaid,* could just as easily be the fish that get eaten" (204). Like his mother, he has been disillusioned, and so they both embrace the more violent versions of fairy tales—the witch being pushed into the oven to burn, the giant falling to his death.

The climax to this story occurs in the restaurant while Phil is quietly seducing the waitress. The narrator overhears a table of very proper, very conventional women expressing their distaste at the Roseanne Barr incident when she grabbed her crotch and spit in true baseball-like fashion after singing the national anthem. The women at the next table excuse men for similar actions because "'A man has to do that'" and "'Men have different needs'" (208, 209). Infuriated by the double standard in life that requires women to act like princesses, the narrator explodes and attacks the women's reasoning with "'What if I *need* to adjust myself? . . . What if I have to keep adjusting my breasts all the time? Let's just say that I can't keep them properly housed inside my bra. What if my butt cheeks just will not stay in place?'" (209). With such an outburst, the narrator ensures that there will be no second date with Phil. She also marks

herself as "the witch." Her final thoughts that night, though, indicate
that she has started to make important changes in herself. She reasons: "And what's wrong with acting out the bad parts? What's
wrong with Jack getting rid of the giant? And why shouldn't Hansel
and Gretel kill the witch in self-defense?" (213). She is finally giving herself permission to be angry, to be less-than-princess, to be the
witch if life so warrants it, and just like a fairy tale, she is giving herself permission to "turn the page and start all over" (213).

"Carnival Lights"

McCorkle's final story in this collection appeared first in *Seventeen* magazine in April of 1992, and it is the story on which
critics seem to have the hardest time agreeing. *The New York
Times Book Review* calls it "possibly the best story" of the collection while *The Georgia Review* lists it as one of the "weaker
stories . . . a meandering, overlong account of a teenage girl's
yearning for her first sexual experience."[11] The truth probably
falls somewhere in between, but it is a troublesome story
because at first glance it does not seem to fit with the other stories in the collection. While most other stories deal with an
adult woman who attempts to pull herself out of a bad situation
by finding her strength, Lori Lawrence seems to have the solu-
tion handed to her, like a winning lottery ticket. With a closer
look, though, the character of Lori does share certain similari-
ties to the other women in *Crash Diet: Stories.*

Lori, a high school senior, is making plans to lose her virginity with her boyfriend, Donnie Wilkins. While planning for

this special night, Lori becomes aware of a terrible secret: Donnie's mother—one of the high school guidance counselors—is having an affair with the high school principal, Mr. Sinclair. In a complicated course of events, Lori chooses to sacrifice her good-girl reputation while never actually having sex in order to cover up the affair and save Donnie from a painful realization about his mother. In addition, her decision calls for her to sacrifice her relationship with Donnie—her erratic behavior causes him to break up with her.

Part of what makes a coming-of-age story is the young adult's recognition that the adult world is not always fair and that adults are not the heroes he/she once believed them to be. The title "Carnival Lights" highlights the illusions Lori believes which must be abandoned in order for her to enter the adult world. As in *Ferris Beach,* the carnival with its Ferris wheel and glittering sideshow attractions symbolize the illusions children may want to believe about life. When Donnie and Lori visit the carnival early on the night they plan their first sexual union, they are filled with expectations and excitement. The moon—a symbol of illusion—"was coming up in the distance," and they talk about visiting several sideshows that offer unbelievable prospects: a fourteen-inch-high horse and a decapitated but still living woman (240). At this point in the evening, Lori is still a believer in romance and love—that is, love connected to sex—but when she learns that Mrs. Wilkins and Mr. Sinclair have been doing exactly what she and Donnie are planning to do, her visions of love and sex as one and the same, pure and sweet, are altered drastically. She feels, rather, like she "might throw up"

(244). All the romantic things she and Donnie say and do to each other seem sordid and shameful when she imagines the illicit lovers doing and saying the same.

Like the other women in *Crash Diet: Stories,* Lori reaches this crisis stage with no initial understanding of how to get through it. At first she seems to work on instinct, dealing with the twisted morality of adult life as best she can. As Elinor Walker points out about all the women in the collection, Lori is "engaged in the process of recreating" herself, but in "Carnival Lights," this is where serendipity comes into play.[12] Mrs. Wilkins and Mr. Sinclair become aware of Lori's knowledge, and they reward her for her silence by giving her a scholarship to the state university. Before the incident they see her only as "'a girl with a grade point total that falls just a little above class average,'" and so they recommend that she take clerical courses at the local technical school rather than pursue her dream to go to college and study architecture or engineering (221).

Lori puts no effort forth to make her dream come true, and yet one would find it difficult to blame her for turning her sacrifice into a chance for success. As Jack Butler notes, Lori "is one of the few who find a way out of their restricted world" with her "liberating disaster." Finally, her sacrifice and reward serve several positive ends. Going to college will make her parents happy, for she sees herself as her "parents' future," just as her parents are taking care of Lori's aging grandfather, and when they stare at her one day, as he does now, with "a blank empty look," she will want to know that despite all her mistakes, she "made at least one decision that was right" (253). This self-sacrificing attitude is clear evidence that Lori is moving toward adulthood and shedding the childish illusions represented by the carnival lights—that she is able to do the right thing in spite of what others think about her and survive in a world where the rules of morality are unclear.

CHAPTER SEVEN

Carolina Moon

A reviewer for *Library Journal* describes the main character of McCorkle's fifth novel, *Carolina Moon,* as "a spider at the center of her web who has wrapped each character in the silken threads that she has cast out."[1] Indeed, the story is very much like a spider's web, plot lines spreading out in different directions, seemingly unrelated, but all woven together in a pattern that is difficult to see unless the reader backs up and views the story at a distance. The dust jacket depicts the tale as "six parallel love stories *and* an unsolved murder mystery," but it would be more accurate to say that the love stories—and the murder—only appear to be parallel; in fact, they intersect and weave together and shoot off in unexpected ways, creating a montage of stories linked by the "spider" in town, Quee Purdy, self-proclaimed free spirit and curator of Fulton, North Carolina's, newest business: Smoke-Out Signals, a clinic for nicotine addicts.[2] The novel was published in December of 1996 and received mixed reviews. While some praised it as "a rollicking tale of love, sex, and addiction in a small Southern town" and a "deeply insightful story of how true community comes out of individuality," others saw it as confusing. In fact, *Carolina Moon* is McCorkle's most sophisticated novel to date, which might help explain some readers' confusion. Within it she works a number of themes, motifs, and images that, like a spider web, all link together to form a fascinating and complex story.

The structure of *Carolina Moon* is reminiscent of two of McCorkle's earlier novels, *July 7th* and *Tending to Virginia*. Like these novels, *Carolina Moon* is told by a variety of different voices, each one revealing secrets, desires, and heartaches. McCorkle explains this structure as "a combination of small pictures. I knew I was working within the framework of a novel, but . . . much of the preliminary work was scene by scene—little vignettes. Then I began to see the common variables that existed between the different characters, and the ways in which they all communicated—or failed to communicate—their lives. . . . What I started to see is that we're all connected by a level of communication we don't really have access to in our everyday lives."[3]

The characters communicate in a variety of ways with varying results, and ironically, although most of the characters yearn for communication and honesty, each is harboring one or more secrets, keeping their true selves hidden. Denny Parks, Quee's newest therapist, dictates her thoughts into a tape recorder, diary-style, to "tell all on these tapes, my life, my secrets" (23). Denny believes falsely that others are drawn to her—she calls herself "a crazy magnet"—but in reality she rarely hears any of the real secrets in the novel, nor does she recognize them as truth when she does hear them. Her move to Fulton comes as a result of her marriage breakup to an English professor whose idea of communication is telling his wife about his research on authors who suffered from allergies. In response to his lack of attention, Denny communicates her desperation by removing her clothes in a public theater, a move which ends the marriage but certainly relays her need for her husband's attention.

Quee, who communicates in several different ways in the novel, has been the topic of local gossip for years. People suspect her of leading a secret life as a witch doctor, a prostitute, or worse, but one of her real secrets is that throughout the years she has performed abortions for frightened, desperate young women in the town. The chapters that focus on Quee's thoughts also include her stories of the pictures she keeps on her wall, and once again McCorkle uses photographs to emphasize the relative truth in such images. Since Quee's childhood, she has been "collecting old photographs" (120). These photos are not of people Quee knows, and other characters are amazed by her ability to create stories for these frozen images. What listeners do not know is that Quee often attaches her own life's stories to these strangers' faces, disguising the truth and allowing herself to "see patterns emerging . . . signs and foreshadowings" in her life by distancing herself, believing "if she could arrange them right they had the power to tell her story, maybe parts that she herself didn't know" (121, 122).

In addition, Quee reveals her thoughts in anonymous letters written to her lover of twenty-five years earlier, Cecil Lowe, Fulton's near-famous writer who eventually killed himself, leaving two fragments of a good-bye note, one found by Quee and the other found by Cecil's son, Tom. Quee writes down her thoughts and mails the letters, addressing them simply to "Wayward One." Ordinarily, these kinds of letters would end up buried along with letters to Santa Claus and God, but what Quee does not know is that her letters are being read by Wallace Johnson, the bored postmaster who is fulfilling his own need for adventure and risk through the letters. Wallace has not told his wife, Judy, about the letters: "In all of the years of their life, this is his only secret. Somehow it seems right that every person *needs* a secret" (8–9). Quee's most shocking secret is the fate of the arrogant and philandering DJ from the local radio station, Jones Jameson, whose body is eventually discovered decaying in a load of topsoil from the riverbank that had been delivered to Myra Carter, widow of Quee's sometimes secret accomplice, Dr. Howard Carter. Quee eventually reveals the truth about Jameson's disappearance in one of the stories she tells about her photographs: that Quee herself murdered Jameson to keep him from revealing the names of those she has aided through abortion.

Connected to the idea of secrets is the role of dreams and illusions in the lives of these characters. In an overview of McCorkle's work, Lynn Bloom notes that one of McCorkle's characters in *Tending to Virginia* learns "salvation lies in a tempered reality rather than in the absolutes of 'always' and 'never.'"[4] This statement could easily describe most of the characters peopling *Carolina Moon,* individuals who feel they cannot live in either complete reality or absolute illusion. Having a dream is a prerequisite to living in Fulton; fulfilling that dream, however, seems near-impossible. Wallace Johnson realizes the anonymous letter-writer is devoting "her whole life to a dream, [spending] all of her time looking to what life was or is going to be" (11). Quee's lover, Cecil Lowe, wrote only one short story, which he entitled "A Dream of Lost Lovers," a fitting title either way it is taken: the fated love affair with Quee which was never to be or the ruined marriage he realized too late was worth saving. McCorkle also tells a story through Wallace Johnson about "Old Lamb's Folly," a huge ship built by a dreamer who realized too late that "there was no possible way to get it out of the clearing and to the sea without cutting down a forest of trees and all the homes that surrounded him." Johnson says it "was a myth, a legend, the kind of thing you can pin a life on if the rest of the world will let you" (104).

Tied closely to the idea of dreams is the idea of a dream house: Tom Lowe's mother dreamed of building the perfect house on her woodland property; Tom's father dreamed of building the perfect beach house before the land was reclaimed by the ocean during Hurricane Hazel; and Sarah McCallister, an unfortunate newlywed who has suffered a brain aneurysm, lies in a coma in the house into which she and her husband Mack moved because it was "her dream" to live there (47). And several times McCorkle relates a story about Quee—who has "had a romance with little houses" since she was a child, hiding underneath her mother's house in her own enclosure, imagining the perfect dream life with the perfect man in a world where she felt powerful, strong, even godlike.

As Sandra Gilbert and Susan Gubar have noted, "enclosure" is one of the key themes in female lives and writing. In houses and in rooms, there is the contradiction of feeling both safe and confined—of being both in a womb and in a tomb. Anxiety about space and the need for escape permeates *Carolina Moon*. On one hand there is Quee, safe within her fantasy house under her mother's house and safe within her pretend house with Cecil Lowe, where she can be his "make-believe wife" (134), but she is also confined by the society in which she lives, marked as an outcast, a witch, a whore, and her victory comes in finding the freedom and movement she needs within the constraints she has been given.

Perhaps the best example of this conflict between claustrophobia and agoraphobia is illustrated in the marriage of Sarah and Mack McCallister. As a young married couple, they should be enjoying life and planning their future as husband and wife, father and mother. Instead, Sarah remains motionless day after day, lying on a bed in her dream house, and Mack feels trapped in a house not of his choosing, able only to imagine guiltily what his life would have been if he had not married her, surrounded by neighbors who represent what he can never have. On one side live college boys, loud and lively, ignorant to life's catastrophes that might await them. On the other side is a pregnant woman and her children, reminding Mack every time he sees her of the family he will never have. He often feels the need to step out on his front porch into the fresh air, even though "Sarah is there, on the other side of the window. Sometimes when he is out here, the wall between them, he can almost forget" (87–88). He is tempted to run away from Sarah and the house, but the end of the novel finds him still watching over her with only a thin line of hope that things will ever change.

Sarah as an apparition haunting Mack's life leads to a number of motifs and symbols McCorkle uses in *Carolina Moon,* the most prominent being ghosts. Ghosts represent the secret parts of people's pasts and presents that they allow to "haunt" them. Sarah haunts Mack's life, and at times he imagines her "rising up behind him like a ghost" (169), but she also is the ghost in Tom Lowe's past. As adolescents, Sarah and Tom loved each other, exploring their sexuality together and eventually going to

Quee for help in erasing their carelessness. Tom has lost Sarah twice, once as a lover and once when she slips into a coma. And here, as in several other situations, McCorkle argues that it is easier to be "'in love with a ghost'" rather than stay in love with a flesh-and-blood, flawed human being.

Quee Purdy, too, is in love with and "haunted" by a ghost, Cecil Lowe (10). Cecil is even described as looking like "a ghost" who is *"haunting* [his] *last spot"* (17, 135). Cecil's suicide is described by detective Robert Bobbin (the same character as in *July 7th*) as "the stuff of old ghost stories," comparing Cecil's suicide using a revolver—which literally blew "his head . . . through the big window and was sliced clean from his neck and the hair on his head"—to another local ghost story teenage boys use to frighten their dates "about a man who searches nightly for his lost head" (115, 177, 125). And like Tom, Quee finds it easier to love a ghost rather than love her husband, Lonnie. Eventually, though, Quee hears the truth about her love affair with Cecil. When her half of the note is joined with Tom's half, she realizes that the note was not written to her, but written to Cecil's wife, telling her that he had never stopped loving her. When Quee realizes that, in fact, she has been in love with nothing, her memories blur and then turn to her husband—yet another ghost by this time—and she begins writing letters to him instead.

Extending the ghost motif, McCorkle plays with the term on several levels. Along with ghost stories of suicide victims, the invisibility of a comatose woman, "haunted" properties of Tom Lowe's childhood, and several characters being described as "being a ghost" or looking like "Casper," Quee names her wall of photographs the "ghost wall." Collecting photographs of other people, to whom Quee assigns "lives and appetites, sex and dreams" (122), is her way to pay "her debt" and care for the "orphaned" souls of the world (14, 122). Haunted by Cecil's suicide, Quee feels the need to pay, perhaps, for Cecil's sin, and so she begins trying to "help others find love and peace and security," whether it means giving an abortion to a frightened teenager or driving a first grader to see the beach for the first time (11).

Closely related to Quee's photograph collection is McCorkle's use of fairy tale imagery in this novel. The oral tradition behind Quee's storytelling is the same tradition found in children's tales—not just the ghost stories mentioned earlier, but the tales of witches and pirates and women in distress. Again, as Gilbert and Gubar have pointed out, the power of fairy tales in our culture is greater than most people would imagine: they "state and enforce culture's sentences with greater accuracy than more sophisticated texts," and because they are told and retold so often to children, their ideas and values are solidly cemented in the subconscious.[5] The adults in this novel are clearly affected by the fairy tales they have heard as children, and their illusions depend upon the simple beliefs that the impossible is possible, good will triumph over evil and be rewarded, and true love will endure.

Along with various references to specific fairy tales such as "Rapunzel," several of the stock characters found in fairy tales show up in *Carolina Moon*. Sarah McCallister is the obvious Sleeping Beauty, but the kiss of her husband will not wake her, and readers are left to wonder if he is her true love; perhaps

Tom Lowe is the one who holds that magic instead. Quee is described by the local residents as "a witch," a "witch doctor," and a "magician" (74, 250)—labels that are "filtered through the safe reign of the parents and into the ears of their children" (250), propagating the fear of anyone who is different. Quee has the delightful eccentric habit of putting "nuggets (pecan, peach pit, golfball)" under the mattresses of her guests—as a way, one assumes, of determining the true nobility of that person as in "The Princess and the Pea" (92). And, as Quee argues, "'Better peas and nuts under mattresses than a cage full of children you're planning to eat, or spindles for people to prick their fingers on, I guess,'" all done in an effort to prove to herself and others "that fairy tales *do* come true" (92).

McCorkle uses several other related motifs and symbols that extend the idea of fairy tales and illusion in general. These motifs—the ocean (which includes stories about the lost city of Atlantis and the sinking of the *Titanic*), pirates, and the moon—overlap and play off each other, exploring the ways people rely upon illusion to help them endure reality. One central image is the ocean, powerful in its pull, unforgiving in its actions. Cecil Lowe's "passion" was the ocean, but his wife rejected it as she "rejected everything of importance" to Cecil (13). It is no wonder, then, that Tom, who like his father is described as having "deep blue" eyes, has conflicting feelings about the ocean (249). It represents his father's dream, and the lot reclaimed by the sea is his birthright, yet like his father, he cannot have the land because the shoreline "takes what it wants to take" (9). The first time Tom and Sarah made love, it was in a river that leads to the ocean, and he admits that for the first time he had found in a person what he gets from the ocean: "a welcoming escape . . . total comfort and safety. He could simply close his eyes and drift, disappear" (127). He later compares their lovemaking (on land) to "being in the middle of the river and unable to touch bottom; a rhythmic treading and gasping and then complete immersion" (130). Sarah even wears ribbons in her hair that are tied in "a sailor's knot" (180), further tying her to Tom's obsession about the ocean.

The movement of the ocean waves represents the rhythm of life, give and take, loss and gain. It is powerful and sometimes frightening, and various characters in the novel struggle with its pull. Before Sarah's aneurysm, she meets Tom in town and attempts to seduce him in an attempt to get pregnant again, since she has been unable to do so with her husband, Mack. Tom looks in her eyes and sees "need" and "a pull like swimming out and then letting go, letting the current pull and pull; there was the fear of drowning in the undertow, forever lost" (142). Tom's instinct is to give himself over to her in the same way he admits that the first time he ever saw the ocean, "his instinct had been to run out into it, to give in and let it pull him, suck him away from the shore" (175). Other characters are also affected by the ocean's pull. Throughout the novel various characters are described in terms such as "drowning," "floating," and "drifting," suggesting their close connection to and control by the power of the waves. To Quee, the ocean lends "perspective," a gift she attempts to share with the children of the town by arranging a field trip to the beach every year for first graders. She remembers seeing the ocean for her very first time and feeling "so small, so helpless in the grand scheme of the world that she decided the only way to survive was to be as strong and powerful as possible" (120). This helps explain Quee's need to control—or maintain the illusion of control over—as much of life as she can. By giving abortions, by curing people of bad habits such as smoking, by choosing to eliminate Jones Jameson, she is attempting to counteract and minimize the power of fate.

Wallace Johnson, the postmaster, perhaps best understands the rhythm of the ocean and its place in the pattern of the world. Wallace is the observer, the overseer, and the commentator on the reader's visit to Fulton. He watches and analyzes without interfering, recognizing the importance of his role: "There's a need for the anchors and the cogs, a need for those who stay in place and mind the shop" (11). He knows that the ocean should "finish what she'd started" and take what shoreline it needed, and he knows he would adjust himself to its needs. As he considers the fate of the Wayward One and the woman he left behind, he wonders how a man could do such a thing to a woman who loved him, especially a man "who had sense enough to understand the power of the moon" in its pull on the tides (108). It is Wallace who has the final word in the novel, a commentary on his future in retirement, spending his days fishing and participating in the rhythm of life rather than fighting against it: "He will spend the next twenty years doing just this, casting and reeling, casting and reeling, casting and reeling with the very movement of the earth" (260).

Tied to this imagery of the ocean are two historical/mythical events—the sinking of the *Titanic* and the lost city of Atlantis—which McCorkle uses dialectically. Atlantis, that legendary utopia, represents all the nurturing aspects of the ocean, and when Tom pictures Atlantis, he pictures "his own town submerged" and safely "swallowed, bottled" (16). The *Titanic,* on the other hand, symbolizes the terrors of the ocean, unexpected tragedy, and imminent death. He imagines the people on the sinking ship who "kept dancing to the orchestra music and drinking," refusing to believe the truth until they threw "themselves out into the icy water, thousands of screams at once" (181). Tom's conflicting feelings about the ocean—and by extension, his father—are symbolized in a dream that includes both the image of Atlantis and the *Titanic.* He sees himself "swimming in the deep" toward Atlantis until he finally "pushes free and swims out into a pure blue bay, a whole world encapsulated there at the bottom of the sea." When he arrives on the white sand, he calls, "I'm home." But the images become confused with noise and distraction, until he sees his father and wonders, "Did his father think of him at all in those minutes [before he killed himself]?" (229). This question refers to an earlier passage describing the sinking of the *Titanic,* in which Tom remembers hearing a story about "a woman whose last memory of her father was his lifting her carefully into a lifeboat." Tom wonders if while waiting to die, this father, as well as Tom's own, thought of his child: "Did he pull out his wallet and show his daughter's picture? Did he think of her at all? Or did he simply embrace death because there was nothing else to embrace?" (182). Tom's father dies feeling betrayed by his romantic vision of nature after Hurricane Hazel destroys his dream of a seaside home, but Tom eventually comes to believe in a balance of the two visions of nature, accepting the advice his father gives to Tom but refuses to take himself: "Tom's father talked about *real* skyscrapers and the way they are built to sway, built to give into nature just enough that they can survive. 'Not a bad code to adopt'" (18).

Because Tom's memories of his father are tied to the sea, he becomes preoccupied with the idea of pirates, perhaps because he feels his father has stolen something from him he can never recover. As a child Tom was told stories by his father about "pirates who once inhabited these very waters" and that their name—Lowe—"was derived from George Lowther's, a pirate from England who killed himself" (16–17). His father's comment on the pirate's suicide is "'It makes sense that he would,'" perhaps explaining Cecil's own choice to end his life: both men had felt their worlds as they knew and loved them had ended. Tom believes that his father's underwater property was "his father's world, a pirate's cove, a treasure chest" (18), and when that was gone, stolen by the sea, his father had nothing else to live for.

Tom makes several further connections between his father and pirates, including comparing his father's death to Blackbeard's: "He fired the pistol and when he did his head went through the big window and was sliced clean from his neck and the hair on his head, the neglected facial hair, burst into flame just like in the story about Blackbeard" (177). The books on his shelves are about "ships and pirates and ghost stories" and even his dogs are named after famous pirates. He calls his collection of dogs his "band of wild dogs," reminiscent of the pirate bands that used to roam the waters around Fulton (23). And although Tom would love to connect somehow with his father through the piracy about which his father told stories, when forced to admit it, Tom knows he "could take the part with the boat and ocean," but what "he couldn't take was the murder" (137). He describes to Quee the pirate superstition about changing fate— "interfering with the underworld" (137). It seems that pirates refused to save their shipmates if they fell overboard, telling them instead, "'Give in, matey, it's meant to be'" (137). Immediately afterward, his thoughts turn to Sarah, deep in a coma, and he knows that if he could have interfered with fate, unlike a true pirate, he would have saved her.

His father, in the form of pirate imagery, continues to haunt Tom's life. While visiting the underwater lot one night, he imagines he hears someone behind him whispering "'Aye, matey, it's a good day to lose your head,'" and he knows that eventually he must come to terms with the loss of his father. Some of the final words Tom says in the novel show his movement toward this acceptance. He admits to Denny that his limited focus has perhaps made him "a ghost" like his father—and like Sarah—and he realizes he must let go of the past in order to have a future: "'I mean, for years now I've been waiting for that famous ship to come in, for the ocean to cough up my land, for somebody to find out my old man left me something after all. But now I know that this is it. I'm it. There is no ship. No treasure'" (241).

It is significant that this novel was the first that McCorkle published after the death of her own father in 1993, and *Carolina Moon* includes many missing fathers and many children coming to terms with that loss in one way or another. In addition to Tom, Denny and Quee also suffer from the lack of a father. Denny's mother told her elaborate lies about her father's success and heroism to hide the fact that her birth was illegitimate and her father abandoned them, and even into her adult life, Denny does not know the truth. Quee's father deserted the family the year she was born, and she admits that she *"never got over wanting* [her] *own daddy"* (106) and felt she had to "stand up for her invisible father" when her mother remarried (120). It is this connection that brings the two women together. As Quee writes in a letter to Denny, "'We are women who spent years missing our fathers and who cling to every story and bit of information we can collect about the men who gave us life'" (27), and unlike Tom, they do not even have submerged land as a gift to remember their ghosts. The connection among Tom, Quee, and Denny is that not any of the three knows the truth about their fathers. Denny continues to believe that her father was "a decorated World War II hero" when she probably "belonged to somebody else's too-hot-for-his-britches step-father" (190), and perhaps her version is not a bad thing to believe. Quee, knowing nothing about her father, constructs elaborate stories for the pictures on her ghost wall, some of them of her and some of complete strangers, giving herself a history. And Tom never finds out the truth about his father's affair with Quee; even when Quee puts the two parts of the suicide note together, she does not tell him the truth. She keeps her secret and allows Tom to believe what he needs to believe about his father, an extension of her mission in Fulton: "help others find love and peace and security," something she believes is more important than the absolute truth (11).

CAROLINA MOON

One final important image in this novel related to truth and illusion can be found its title: *Carolina Moon.* The title comes from a song by the same name, and the words describe an ideal lover waiting faithfully: "Carolina Moon, keep shining, / Shining on the one who waits for me," much as Quee remains loyal to her memories of Cecil until she is confronted with the absolute truth about his feelings for her. In the novel the title appears on a sign in one of Quee's photos, showing a young girl at the beach who, according to Quee's story, has just fallen in love. The girl sees in this man "the promise that this may very well be her ticket out of her present life and into another" (223). In Quee's story, in contrast to her real experience with Cecil, the woman eventually ends up with the man, both leaving the people to whom they are married. The moon, an image McCorkle uses in *The Cheer Leader, Ferris Beach,* and various short stories as well, is McCorkle's strongest symbol of the illusions people live with and prefer to believe: moonlight is romantic and forgiving, and under its light it is easier to imagine an ideal life. In one of Quee's letters to "Wayward One," she remembers a morning on the beach with Cecil and his romantic interpretation of the moon: "*It was almost a full moon and you talked about how even though you knew that there was a flag up there on it, and that men had landed and walked and taken close-up photos that appeared in* Life *magazine, you still felt complete magic when you looked at it*" (107). Even though at the time Quee believes his "*every brilliant word,*" she later realizes that such romantic visions of life and idealized love must be tempered with reality in the same way the moon—or illusion—controls the tides of the oceans—the rhythm of daily living.

Carolina Moon is about more than the conflict of romance and reality, however. It is about the lack of control people have over their lives and the lengths they will go to convince themselves otherwise. Because Quee is at the center of the novel, it is her own struggle against fate that plays the biggest part in the story. When Quee hears Tom read the missing part of his father's suicide note, she realizes that Cecil was writing a farewell love note not to her but to his wife, expressing regret that he did not realize his love for Tom's mother earlier. When Tom comments that his mother never wanted to read the note, not caring whether her husband loved or hated her, Denny remarks, "'I'd want to know, wouldn't you?'" Quee's reply to this sums up her resistance to painful truth; she says, "'No, I don't think I would'" (248). Instead of accepting truth and facing reality, Quee has spent her life ignoring it, twisting it, and trying to alter it. Her abortions rewrite a couple's history, giving them a second chance at determining their futures; she revisions the people in her photos, giving them the life she desires for them; her clinic gives people a second chance to overcome destructive habits; and her letters to Cecil attempt to continue a relationship ended by death. In one of those letters, she admits that sometimes she "*play[s] God,*" and she describes herself as a child under her house leaning up against the "*lattice work*" as a "*spider in a web*" spinning "*cottony threads*" that bind others in a cocoon. Such images of restraint and enclosure illustrate the power Quee feels over the lives of others, seeing it as her duty and privilege to control their fates.

Quee is not the only character hitting her head against the hard wall of fate. The saddest story in the novel concerns Mack and Sarah, and it is the one story that seems to hold no hope. At the end of the book, Sarah is still in a coma, Mack has rejected her best friend June as a "replacement" for his wife, and his future appears to be an endless series of days and nights, tending to his motionless wife. His life seems similar to the game he watches the neighborhood children play—freeze tag—during which random children who have been "tagged" must stand frozen like statues while others run free (232). In an on-line interview with Ballantine Reader's Circle, McCorkle sums up *Carolina Moon* as "a collection of people who have reached a point in life where the situation they're in is completely out of their control. They've basically come to a point where the only way to survive is to reach a level of acceptance." McCorkle's comments seem especially appropriate to Mack, who must struggle against his fate before accepting that he cannot change things. If Sarah were either to die or to wake up by the end of the novel, McCorkle would be including a sort of deus ex machina that simply does not exist.

Myra Carter, the doctor's widow who finds Jones Jameson's body in her recently delivered topsoil, sums up McCorkle's message about fate: "But life doesn't always give you a choice. Life might just say: Here's your old gummed-up hand, now play it! Life might say: Here's your topsoil, and we threw a dead man in for good measure. It might say: Here's your husband you love so dearly, and now he's gone" (237). Having faced both truth and illusion, McCorkle's characters in this novel, as in her earlier ones, are able to move forward—quickly or in small steps—having decided for themselves what illusions they need to survive and which ones they can live without.

CHAPTER EIGHT

Final Vinyl Days and Other Stories

McCorkle's seventh book is her second book of short stories, *Final Vinyl Days and Other Stories,* published in June of 1998.[1] As with her earlier collection, *Crash Diet: Stories,* this book is "chock full of New South eccentrics, comic moments and perplexing situations," and like her earlier stories, her witty humor thinly veils the tragedy in nearly every story. Reviews of *Final Vinyl Days* were generally very positive; one reviewer even claims that "McCorkle is gradually becoming our contemporary Eudora Welty."[2] High praise, indeed.

McCorkle uses a variety of voices in this collection, speaking from both male and female points of view, the stories held together by similar thematic threads—threads somewhat reminiscent of *Crash Diet: Stories.* As Donna Seaman notes in her review for *Booklist,* the stories all deal with "how people cope with the boons and forfeitures of life." Beyond that, however, the stories shoot off in various directions, as mainly dysfunctional people bang their heads against the reality set before them. As the book jacket notes, the characters are all "traveling off the beaten path"—and it is clear none of them has brought a map. Their stories, as *The New York Times Book Review* describes them, are often "exasperating cases," and while the stories do not always conclude with protagonists gaining insight, the reader nearly always does, often realizing "some truths you didn't realize you knew."[3]

The novel's epigraph is a line from Marvin Gaye's song "If I Should Die Tonight": "How many hearts have felt their world stand still?" Each character in these stories finds her/himself at a juncture, a moment of questioning or decision-making when life has seemed suddenly to "stand still." And each one handles that moment differently, some forging through, some stalling out. The stories are grouped in three parts, each containing three stories—two in first-person and one in third-person limited. The first three stories show characters struggling with accepting a good situation, sure that things will go terribly wrong. Each protagonist in this part, however, eventually accepts—sometimes grudgingly—that happiness is possible. Part 2 is less optimistic. The three main characters in these stories do not, by the stories' ends, move forward. Perhaps there is hope, but for the moment they remain hampered by their fears. Part 3 returns to the affirmation found in the first three stories. While all three stories deal with serious subjects, in the end the protagonists triumph in some way, no matter how small the victory may appear to others.

Part One

"Paradise"

"Paradise," also published in *New Stories From the South, 1996* and *Chattahoochee Review,* is a whimsical story of a man and woman—named Adam and Eve—who meet at a wedding, fall into bed together, and in spite of their cynicism about the probability of success, fall into love and eventually marriage.

McCorkle has great fun with the Biblical allusions: other characters make many jokes about "a rib or a snake. Apples. Fig leaves" and whether or not they have navels (17), and after they marry, Adam muses about the possibilities of living in a town somewhere called Eden, meeting each other "on the sixth day," and naming their first child "Cain" (33). Adam also keeps thinking Eve "should be the one initiating" discussions of marriage, knowing, like the first Adam, that he would prefer to be "the innocent man . . . the ruined man," forced by fate into marrying her (32–33). Beneath the jokes, though, lies the question most people ask about love in today's world: Is there still a chance of finding Paradise and living happily together forever? Or are people destined to "fall" out of love eventually and, like Adam's parents, divorce?

McCorkle uses many polarities in this story—contrasts of culture, geography, and personality as well as more philosophical differences between the two main characters, creating two very unlikely soul mates, and unlike their Biblical namesakes, they appear to have a choice about their partners for life. Adam was raised in New York City, lives in Washington, D.C., and is Jewish and a Yankee. Eve is from a small southern town, lives in Atlanta, and is Protestant. Love and the instinct to join one's life with another prevails, however, and obstacles seem less important than being together.

When the story begins at a friend's wedding, Adam is wondering how yet another one of his fraternity brothers can be exchanging single life for a clichéd wedding and marriage: "The price of freedom was exorbitant these days. So why was everyone biting the hook? Why were these reasonably intelligent, likable guys *choosing* to acquiesce, their suppressed desires left to blow up at some occasional wedding party" (11). The wedding is a familiar one—no matter what the region—and one can almost hear the Stage Manager from Thornton Wilder's classic American drama *Our Town* saying, "only one in a hundred is interesting.'" *Our Town*'s Stage Manager also said, however, that "People are meant to live two by two," a philosophy that Adam has yet to believe or accept. Adam's own insecurities brought about by his parents' divorce after more than thirty years of marriage and his fears of falling into the rut of traditional life make him resistant to love, but in the end he knows he "has no good reason," and that this "rare match . . . might never happen again" (29).

McCorkle satirizes many aspects of love, marriage, and southern life in this tale. The people at the wedding rarely put substance above appearance: the bridesmaids get Retin-A as party favors, the women are more concerned with getting Yard of the Month than in loving their neighbors, and the marriages are "walking advertisements for Talbots and Brooks Brothers" (9). When one of the groomsmen passes out during the ceremony (due to effects still felt from the bachelor party the night before), rather than interrupt the ceremony, someone from the congregation simply "checked his pulse and then rolled him under the front pew" (10). The result is that readers (and Adam and Eve) are both drawn to and repelled by such sentimental and traditional rituals. The truth McCorkle reveals is that when someone is not emotionally involved, love, weddings, marriage, and family life seem mawkish, but when that same someone falls in love, such things seem worth the trade-off. Once

Adam lowers his guard and lets himself admit his feelings about Eve, he becomes the total romantic. Their wedding closely resembles the one where they first meet, they settle into a life similar to his fraternity brothers, and his future stretches into "subdivisions, and cocktail parties, fields, forests, temptations and promises" (34). "Ain't love grand?" McCorkle seems to ask. Next to love, all else pales in comparison.

"Last Request"

The second story in *Final Vinyl Days* centers around a mother's deathbed request that her daughter, Tina, remain married "no matter what happens, no matter how lousy your life becomes" (35). Tina's twin sister, Twyla, who is already divorced, receives no similar supplication, and so Tina is left to wonder why she has been singled out to fulfill her mother's dying wish.

Twyla is Tina's alter ego, and as with other such pairings in McCorkle's work, Twyla is allowed to do and say the things Tina is not: Tina is "so smart, so capable, so solid and dependable—great childbirthing hips," but Twyla is the "recently divorced, let's-have-a-party kind of sibling" in a "wee petite body" (36–37). While Tina dresses in a "Sunday school outfit" and sings "'The Lord's Prayer' in the high school talent show," Twyla wears a man's suit, slicks back her hair, and sings "Take a Walk on the Wild Side" (37–38). The men they choose to marry reflect their extreme differences, as well. Tina marries the safe Doug—"*a little plain and dull and ordinary,*" according to her mother— while Twyla marries the flashy Ronald, "a lawyer who wore a lot of jewelry" (41). The quality of Tina's life seems obvious to the reader, yet Tina herself cannot see that her life is infinitely better than Twyla's—although perhaps less like a ride on a roller coaster. A large part of Tina's problem can be traced to her mother, a strong woman who simultaneously represents inflexibility and stability. Tina sees her as a woman who never changes, who is "even in death . . . the most stubborn person" she had ever met (45). And when her mother grips her hand and makes her last request, Tina is sure it is because her mother knows "something about Doug" that is so bad, she knows only this deathbed promise will keep her married to him because "never had she pushed me in the right direction. Never had she given me good advice" (37).

Tina's mother has suffered from her own bad marriage and is, in fact, trying to make sure that at least one female in the family has a successful marriage. McCorkle offers evidence that both Tina's mother and father had extramarital affairs, and when her father died—demolished in the rubble of a tornado—he was at his mistress's apartment, "bathing in the afterglow of . . . whatever" (56). Tina has her own childhood memory of her mother, leaning into a "big man with hair that ran down his neck," her hands "pressing the front of his trousers" (52). With such a family make-up, it is no wonder that Tina feels suspicious about her mother's advice. McCorkle uses a great deal of imagery associated with laundry—soap, dirty and clean clothing, washing machines and dryers—as symbolic reference to "clean" and "dirty" practices of Tina's parents and other married people. Tina's memory of her mother with her lover is standing "in front of the washing machine" (52), for example. Her father was a fireman, always coming home with "soot on his belongings," dirt that no laundry detergent could remove, and as her mother states, "'Those stains were symbolic'" (44). Her mother also collects samples of "soap, shampoo, toothpaste," but never actually uses them: "she just liked to possess them, save them, count them" (43). Perhaps her mother never uses the soaps because she could never clean up her marriage—or was afraid if she forced her husband to change, she would have to admit her own downfall, or perhaps she saved these "travel sizes" with the intention of one day breaking away and leaving. The "dirty laundry" motif continues: Tina's mother first discovers her husband's infidelity by finding another woman's "Lee press-on nail clinging to his underwear" (51) when she is loading the washer. In turn, after her mother dies, Tina's suspicions that her mother knew something about Doug lead to her own foray through the laundry: "I sniffed all of his clothes in the hamper to see if I could smell quick afternoon sex" (49).

Truth is a painful but necessary awakening for the characters in this story. Tina remembers her father taking the family out to the country to see the fascinating results of a lightning strike: "a huge oak tree in the middle of a tobacco field, split through the middle with a precise blackened stroke," but he also shows them the "cows, their stiff frozen legs sticking out from them" and the flies "in a thick black swarm." He points with authority at the bull who had survived by not seeking shelter beneath the tree with the cows. Although the father is proud that the male lived by watching out for himself, the mother bitterly points out that he will probably "'just hop off to a new pasture and start over,'" and Tina notes that the bull is "grazing in a death field" (54). Fittingly, Tina's father is killed by a similar storm, this time as the bull that does not escape.

Tina sees her mother's last words as a "hex" upon her, but the final page of "Last Request" brings together the images in the story with an affirming ending not unlike "Paradise." After visiting her mother's grave, Tina heads home, but notices there are "dark clouds gathering." Doug is out playing golf, and she thinks "of that old bull grazing in his field," her "father more or less grazing in *his* field," and "Doug walking from tee to tee, the tallest thing on the green—a warm-blooded lightning rod." Suddenly Tina realizes she does not want her husband to experience a similar fate. Her most important insight is that she finally understands that her mother asked her to stay with Doug not because he was worth leaving, but because he was worth keeping. In fact, her mother "wanted a man like Doug" herself (58). Her last advice to her daughter is her best.

Tina finally sees that Doug is "a man smart enough to come in out of the rain," and the final image in the story is of clean laundry and circle imagery as their clothes tumble in the dryer, "warm and dry when the cycle reached its end" (58). Like Adam in "Paradise," Tina resists believing that true love could exist and endure because of the mistakes of her parents, but she learns that in spite of the negative possibilities, love is worth pursuing and fighting for.

"Life Prerecorded"

The last story in part 1 is a monologue by a woman known only as "Mrs. Porter," a southerner who has moved to Boston.

Throughout the story, she offers glimpses of her childhood, her pregnancy, the birth, and motherhood. Events of the past and present are woven together with her dreams, which often reflect her wishes as well as her fears. The title refers to the idea that no life is completely different but is a repetition of those who have come before, the cycles all lives follow: life/death, youth/age, innocence/experience.

During the narrator's pregnancy, she faces her own mortality, realizing that she will no longer be the child but rather be the protector of the child. Nothing will ever be the same because her life will no longer be her own; she will be responsible for the life of another, and her "sins" affect more than herself. She is a smoker and drinker but knows that she must stop because the doctor has frightened her into visions of a "blackened placenta slipping onto a clean hospital floor" (61). The responsibility of taking care of a child seems a "burden," and her dreams are full of memories of grandmothers, mothers of friends—many who have died—signaling her own worry that she will not live to raise her child. She also has the occasional strange dream that her child will not be normal—born a kitten or even handed to her in freeze-dried form.

People of every generation fill this story—children and memories of children, young mothers, elderly people—all at different stages of life but all of whom will follow to some degree the "prerecorded" pattern of existence. When the narrator goes to a clinic to confirm her pregnancy, there are others waiting, too, not all of them as happy to get positive results. On the other hand, her elderly friend, Joseph, shares sweet memories of his wife, Gwendolyn, and their childless years of happiness together. Joseph's character plays an important role in the narrator's life. He tells her that he is her "future," and he is also a representative of wisdom. He literally wears many hats, purchasing a new one each season, marking the ongoing movement of time. In addition, each season he "purges"—that is, he "gathered up everything he could live without and took it [to] the Salvation Army bin" (65). Similarly, the world periodically purges itself—out with the old and in with the new.

Her memories and dreams focus on times of innocence as a child and a teenager—"before Martin Luther King was shot . . . when Elvis still walked the rooms of Graceland . . . when my sister was practicing to be a cheerleader, and my grandmother was still walking the rows of her garden" (76)—before she recognized her own mortality. She smokes without fearing death; she drives in fast cars with friends, feeling "powerful"; and she avoids cemeteries where the grave markers are too recent because "it all seemed to close" (92, 89). Her memories also pinpoint the moments when bits of innocence are lost: smoking cigarettes in secret, the "monumental corner" of her first period, "the height of first love, Saturday nights in parked cars or on the busted couch of somebody's forsaken game room" (84, 85), discovering she is pregnant, giving birth, and watching that child start on the same cycle of experience.

The pivotal moment of giving birth to her daughter marks the moment when the narrator moves into the next stage of life. She is not like Joseph—facing imminent death—but she can no longer be the child in her memories, even though at times she imagines she still can "find a clean path into my childhood where I might race my bike, down the street and into the yard, the wheels spinning and clicking—a triangle cut from an aluminum pie pan clothes-pinned to a spoke" (87). The final image in the story shows her five-year-old daughter dressed in adult clothes and high heels, pretending a pencil is a cigarette, blowing smoke her mother's way. And while the narrator knows she can never really relive childhood, she can experience the innocence of childhood again through her daughter, and so she leans "close to breath it all in" (93).

PART TWO

"Final Vinyl Days"

In "Final Vinyl Days" McCorkle moves into uncharted territory for her—that is, speaking with the voice of a man. The young unnamed male protagonist in this title story is a misfit in the modern world, living "in the scratchy grooves of the past" before compact discs brought on the death of the vinyl record. He gauges his life and loves by pop music, using it as a reference guide. The day his girlfriend Betts moves in, for example, is "1984, the day after Marvin Gaye died" (97). He also judges others by their choice of music and dismisses potential lovers if they listen to music he dislikes. He even justifies being with his girlfriend Betts by referring to music: she is "short on sense of humor but long on legs. Sometimes you buy an album for just one song, thinking that the others will start to grow on you" (99).

Like the records he treasures, the narrator "await[s] extinction" because modern life has no place for someone or something so out of step (114). The women in his life constantly try to steer him onto the rat track for success, encouraging him to go to law school, to graduate school, or to take up the family business. And just like one of his idols, Marvin Gaye—who was killed by his own father— the narrator fears being "killed" by the ones who love him. And so he resists and eventually loses every woman with whom he develops a relationship. Living in the past is much easier than facing reality, and so he continues playing the part of alien in his own world, a victim of the forward movement of time. He compares himself to the single goldfish swimming around in a cloudy aquarium in the doctor's office: "the only son of a bitch on the planet, thirty gallons of water and nobody to swim over and talk to" (106).

Over and over, the narrator sabotages his own chances at happiness. It is not merely that he feels a generational gap with today's youth; he feels alienated from every generation. Betts is younger than he is, and he claims they are "from different time zones" and that there is "a real bad connection" between them (99, 101). His mother calls him on the phone, asking about his plans for employment, and he turns on the blender and pleads "bad connection" (100). And finally, with Marlene, a childhood friend who "*has possibly heard some songs from* [his] *youth,*" he gives up so easily, chanting "Bad connection, bad connection" (107, 111). Clearly, the narrator cannot make a connection to anyone, and that keeps him less vulnerable. Everything about the past seems ideal and romantic to him, but his nostalgia is paralyzing, and he blames all his difficulties on the fact that society continues to move forward.

Unlike the three stories in part 1, "Final Vinyl Days" embodies a wistfulness that leaves the reader feeling sad for a variety of reasons. Although he acknowledges some advantages to modern living as an adult, such as recycling, environmentalism, and a paycheck, he focuses on the disadvantages, such as young people seeking individualism in ways he does not understand, women who expect him to do more than work in a used record store, and Marvin Gaye's music set to "fat raisins dancing around on the tube" (120). He is a purist in the worst sense of the word, expecting everyone else to live by his standards. McCorkle offers little hope at the end of this story. The narrator is still working at the record store, still alienated from his family and women, and still having only fantasies about a happy life. And until he faces life as it is now instead of life as it was, he will continue to flounder, living in a world like the cover of the Joni Mitchell album, looking "out on the dreary day" (118).

"Dysfunction 101"

McCorkle continues the dysfunctional trend of part 2 with this story (the shortest in the collection) about a woman trying to extricate herself from a debilitating upbringing. The unnamed narrator was raised by her grandmother, a woman who ended her own marriage by threatening to kill her husband "if he didn't take to the road and never return" (129). Her mother was "too young to be a mother" and "wanted a chance in life" and so left her daughter to her own mother's care (124). "Such is my legacy," the narrator laments, and she then spends the rest of her time trying to recover from such rough beginnings.

McCorkle includes an alter ego character named Mary Edna, a woman with an equally sad childhood but one who has chosen to react in a different way than the narrator. Mary Edna seems to revel in her dysfunctional background. Even as children, when the narrator winces and recoils from the negative label, Mary Edna "grinned and waved at everybody like she might have been the homecoming queen" because she believed "any attention is better than nothing" (123). While the narrator stays at home and baby-sits Mary Edna's two children—hoping to give them "a spine of steel"—Mary Edna visits Roy's Holiday Lounge and dances with out-of-towners. The narrator knows that each generation pays for the "sins" of the mothers and fathers—especially the mothers, it seems. She calls it the "chain reaction of mamas" and states that "everybody is trying so hard to make up for her mama's failures" (124). She also knows, however, that the chain can be broken, and that is her hope for herself as well as for Mary Edna's daughters.

The illusion vs. reality conflict so prevalent in McCorkle's work evidences itself in this story as well. The narrator has always believed that she and Mary Edna would "grow up to catch the world by its tail like a comet," but now she wonders "what on earth happened" (123). Dreams of childhood remain dreams as the narrator gradually comes to understand the difficulty in overcoming the obstacles she inherited. When she was a child, she would create "wonderful romantic adventures" for the mother she had never met, but in reality, when she finally meets her mother, she finds a dirty, obese woman who has spent her life moving from one bad relationship to another. Although her grandmother's advice is usually harsh, she does lead the narrator toward an understanding of the difference between dreams and reality: She warns her granddaughter that "'things ain't always as they look, sound, or smell'" (127). The narrator recounts a survey, which supports her grandmother's advice, in which foreigners were given a list of English words and asked to select which word "sounded most lovely." Ninety percent of the people chose "diarrhea," a fact which makes the narrator laugh and admit "you just can't count on anything to be as it appears" (127). She seems to understand that it is sometimes necessary to lie "as a form of survival" (131), to temper reality with some dreams.

The dirty/clean imagery McCorkle uses in "Last Request" appears also in "Dysfunction 101." The narrator wants life to be "clean, sober" (129), but when she meets her mother, her mother's toenails look "like she'd been digging potatoes." Rather than agreeing with Mary Edna—that painting one's toenails can cover up such dirt—the narrator wants to shout at her mother, "'Liberate yourself—shed that filth and pestilence'" (129). One of her wishes is to give her mother "a case of Ivory soap and thick nubbly washcloths to cleanse herself" (132). The narrator has also rejected men for lack of cleanliness—one for smelling "like a chicken" and another for having gingivitis (130). She loves to floss her teeth, taking the "pulpy, unhealthy gums" and flossing them "until they are tough and ready, no longer bleeding" (131). Her desire is to do the same thing metaphorically to the children she teaches—making them tough enough to overcome whatever has made them "bleed."

As in "Final Vinyl Days," McCorkle offers no happy ending, but there is hope for the narrator. She has a plan—a primer, in effect, for overcoming a dysfunctional past, as the title suggests. Her first step is to "recognize what was wrong." In other words, one must acknowledge obstacles—something Mary Edna has not done but what the narrator accomplishes with this monologue. Second, she believes one must "*accept* it" as the truth, rather than trying to live in illusion. Finally—tied to her dirty/clean imagery—she says one must "walk off and leave it there; it is not your mess to clean up" (132), suggesting that while she would like to "clean up" her mother, she knows that no one can do that except her mother. Like the woman in her earlier collection of stories, *Crash Diet: Stories,* this narrator has come up against real adversity but is trying, through her own spunk and determination, to transcend the life she has been handed.

"A Blinking, Spinning, Breathtaking World"

The final story in part 2 centers around Charlotte, a woman recently separated from her husband and caring for her young son, Sam. Since her husband left her, the world has become a very frightening place, a "blinking, spinning, breathtaking world" that feels horribly out of control, violent, and dangerous. When she was young, she loved experiences such as carnival rides that took her breath away and made her temporarily frightened. She first met her husband, Jeff, at a haunted car wash—a place they returned every year to celebrate their meeting—and on her honeymoon she and Jeff "had ridden a rollercoaster that raced upside down through a dark tunnel," laughing "at the sign warning those with heart problems to stay away" (143). But now Charlotte is suffering from a different kind of "heart" problem, and she wants no more dangers, either real or imagined.

Charlotte is an extremely careful woman, a woman who has supplies stored for every emergency, a woman whom her husband nicknamed *"the liberal survivalist"* (136). It is a fitting name, for Charlotte approaches every moment in life as if it were a survival test. She has a car alarm, she considers writing down where she parks when she takes Sam to a children's amusement center, and she has to stop herself from "repeatedly checking [the safety bars on the rides] lifting and pulling . . . the same way she did the doors and windows of their house late at night" (144). Even her job—a technician who prepares people for MRIs—puts her in the position of warning other people about the discomfort they might encounter. By being fully prepared, by being on alert at all times, Charlotte hopes to avoid risk and assuage her fears. Her main goal in life at this point is survival, no matter what it takes. Despite the emergency items in her basement, she admits that "there were no survival kits" for what had happened to her and her marriage. Friends who have tried to offer comfort have been rejected because she "was afraid to trust anybody" (138–39, 147).

Everything seems to scare Charlotte at this point in her life. McCorkle uses the words "fear" and words that connote fear such as "scared" and "afraid" over and over in the story. Charlotte reviews stories in the news about normal people who suddenly snap, who murder their families in hideous ways, who attack people in parking lots, who kidnap innocent children. She has become nearly paranoid as she looks around, believing one cannot tell a good person from a bad one. She admits fearing "extremes," believing that if things are too good, they cannot stay that way, and if things are too bad, she feels "overwhelmed by the energy required to climb back up." What she wants is stability—to live "right in the middle." Nature reflects her fears in this story: It is spring, but bitter cold with a blizzard on the way. The cold "sets her teeth on edge" and knots her muscles (134). Even the crocus bulbs refuse to reach up and break out of the soil. The interior of the children's amusement center—with a motif of Alice in Wonderland—also mirrors her state of mind. Like Alice, Charlotte is experiencing a surrealistic twist in her life. The mirrored funhouse makes everyone appear distorted, the Mad Hatter's tea-party ride seems dangerous, and the rabbit hole through which Charlotte (and Alice) must slide to enter Wonderland is especially threatening. Children adore it, but Charlotte sees it as "a huge twisting slide through darkness" (141), and although she "lets the tube take her body," she screams all the way to the bottom, arriving tense and breathless (143).

Symbolically, she knows she has "reached the bottom of the long dark hole" in her life as well, and her only choices are either to "remain there or begin working her way back to the surface." Unlike Alice, Charlotte has "no magic potion; no incantation to make the world stop blinking, stop spinning." And as the story ends, like the two other protagonists from the stories in part 2, Charlotte is still paralyzed, knowing what she must do to survive, but still "scared frozen, scared to death" (155).

PART THREE

"Your Husband Is Cheating on Us"

This amusing story first appeared in *Oxford American*. It is a first-person narration spoken by the "other woman," who has found out that her lover is cheating on both her and his wife, and so she goes to tell the wife and to suggest they kill him together. Although McCorkle does not supply the wife's comments, it is obvious that the encounter is face-to-face. The mistress says, "Don't look at my hair" and "Truth is you look a far sight better than how he painted you" (161, 164), and the wife responds both verbally and nonverbally as indicated by the mistress's words: "The baby? You're asking about *my* baby?" and "Oh, my, stop crying" (164, 171).

Although the one-sided conversation is about the *other* other woman, the story reveals much more about the mistress and wife, who both elicit sympathy, and the husband, who does not. The unnamed narrator and mistress has accepted her place as "test wife" and seems proud of the fact that the husband has been faithful to her for eight years. Her self-esteem, however, is suspect because when she compares herself to the wife, she says the wife would be "the fair, hothouse flower" and she would be "the scrub grass by the side of the road" (159). Atypically for a mistress, she is older than the wife and larger in size. She has struggled in life, lost a baby, and acknowledges that she is "a quitter": when "the going gets tough," she gets "the hell out" (160).

She claims to have "pride" and "dignity," perhaps ironic for a woman in her position, but because of the difficult life she has led, she has developed her own brand of ethics—and a strange affinity with the woman whose husband she shares. As her eight-year affair has progressed, she has come to know the wife almost intimately— her perfume, her voice on the answering machine, her personal tragedies, her menstrual cycle, and her smoking habits—and thus her loyalties have shifted. The husband becomes a target for her anger and the wife becomes her ally. He is not worthy of either woman, the mistress believes. The woman he has chosen as his new mistress is the stereotypical Other Woman: "much younger" with "boobs . . . you could place a cafeteria tray" on, who wears "shorts skirts" and "over the knee boots" and too much makeup. Such a vulgar and ordinary choice disgusts the mistress who sees herself and the wife as "two perfectly good-hearted, good-looking women" (169) who have been betrayed.

Although this story is amusing in ironic and surprising ways, again McCorkle seems to be making a larger statement: women must stick together. By having an affair with a married man, a woman becomes disloyal to her own sex, injuring a "sister" who might just turn out to be herself one day. Below the humor is a feminist statement—and the suggestion of murder by arsenic or cyanide in baked goods or smothering him in his bed puts teeth into that statement. Unlike the characters in part 2, this woman is taking control of her life, using any method she has at her disposal.

"It's a Funeral! RSVP"

In 1993 McCorkle's father was dying, and it was during this difficult period that she first came up with the idea for this story. At the same time, McCorkle's aunt was dying, and she noticed that the two of them approached death in very different ways—her father speaking in metaphors and her aunt "telling everyone exactly how and what she wanted done" at the funeral. Because she knew her father's death was fast approaching, McCorkle had the chance to say the things she wanted to say before he died, and she began to think that preparing for one's own death, even going to one's own funeral—"the old Tom Sawyer thing"—would be great because one would "have a little control there."[4]

The narrator of "It's a Funeral! RSVP" is a woman who makes this possible for others by "*throw*[ing] *funerals*" (173). She is one of McCorkle's spunkiest women, someone who does things like "chug, eat huge desserts, hug and kiss perfect strangers who look like they need some attention" (178). The humor in this story is of the classic black kind—that is, humor about subjects ordinarily not considered funny. McCorkle knows that no matter what happens in life, including death, "life just doesn't stop."[5] Such a philosophy about life and death is necessary in the line of work the narrator has chosen. She has seen enough death to know that everyone needs an "aid to the other side. A hand to hold" (188). Her service includes planning out funerals, complete with hymns and speeches, burial plans, and messages to those left behind.

Most important, however, is her gift for getting "folks as close as possible to what means the most in this life" (191), for what she does best is comment on the lives people lead before they die—and this is the real strength of the story. When facing death, people often reevaluate their lives, finding regrets in previous behavior. A predeath funeral allows the dying to "clear the air" with enemies, show love and forgiveness, change attitudes—such as the woman whose funeral is attended by no one, so she "write[s] letter and notes and make[s] phone calls" before having a second funeral, which is "a full house" (190). Her comments at the second funeral show real growth that might not have occurred otherwise: She says, "'Why . . . did I waste my time being such a godawful bitch?'" (190–91).

By facing death in her business, the narrator has scrutinized her own life as well as others'. She has become very philosophical—yet very practical. She knows that what matters is not whether your children "speak one language or three," read *Time* or the *New Republic,* or do any number of activities that reflect more upon their parents than upon the children; what matters are the things children and dogs have taught her—and "it is simple" (179). The best things in life include children stretching "out in the sunshine with their bookbags tossed off to the side," peeing out in the open air, sniffing "the good pure air and stretch[ing] out in a puddle of sunshine," and especially being open to "spirits and waves of emotions" that adults often ignore (178, 196, 181). The final lessons that this woman, nicknamed "the Mistress of Death" by some people in her town, has to offer are about both life and death. No matter what the circumstances or the cause of death, no matter what religious beliefs the dying may or may not have, she knows that they "are reassured that things in life do matter—every day, every word, every strain of music, every little gust of wind that stirs the branches" (192). The other lesson—about death—is spoken by a man whose mind "was cloudy with morphine and fatigue," who spoke about death by using a metaphor about a new tax law: "this new law dealt with each and every person in the exact same way; there is no distinction or special consideration for any one group over another one. He said if the laws are working and people are feeling hopeful, then that is good—trust them, believe in them, stick with them—oh, but if you see that they are not going to work, then you have to accept that. You have to embrace that truth and then find another way to go" (196–97).

Such words of wisdom concerning, in part, the equality of death—that no one is overlooked or treated special—is a reminder to all the living to be, like the narrator, always "prepared to see death" (188), making for fewer regrets when the inevitable occurs.

"The Anatomy of Man"

The final story in part 3 and in the book is perhaps the most difficult to characterize in terms of the other stories in *Final Vinyl Days*. In "The Anatomy of Man" McCorkle has written a third-person limited narrative from the perspective of a young pastor who is struggling with his profession, his seemingly mystical abilities, and his sexual fantasies about women. As he contemplates his life, he floats in a warm baptismal pool, stretched out in a position reminiscent of Leonardo da Vinci's drawing that serves as the title to the story.

The pastor has an uncle who also has strange abilities: he claims he can "see germs lit up like infrared," and so his family has him institutionalized in a place that gives him "heavy medication and arts and crafts lessons" (199, 200). This uncle seems to believe that his nephew also has certain abilities. And he does. The pastor can sense sadness, can sense impending disease, can even hear voices, but because he has seen how his family reacted to his uncle, he "knew better as a child than to tell anyone" (199). Ironically, his gift is not questioned because he is attached to conventional religion, and McCorkle leaves the reader wondering why mysticism is accepted only under those circumstances.

He also struggles with his worldly desires to have a "normal" life. The only women his congregation members introduce to him are the "*good girls,*" but the women "who spark his blood" shy away from him, no doubt of a different type (199, 202). His fantasies include a woman from his church who "appears at the baptismal in a white bikini" wearing blood red toenail polish the color of communion wine, with skin as white as "unleavened wafers" (203), clearly a combination of good and evil, sensuality and innocence, and an indication of the conflict he is feeling about his profession. After all, as the title states, the pastor is a man, not a god, with the demanding anatomy of one, and McCorkle could be implying that people might expect too much from such a man. He is even unable to sustain the fantasy; his ability to see her sadness and hear the sickness around him moves him away from his physical desires.

The ending of the story is affirming, however, and this is what links it to the other two stories in part 3. Even as he struggles to define himself in his calling, he hears his uncle's voice in his head telling him, "*If you don't do something . . . your beliefs are worthless*" (211). Then the voice becomes real, and he actually hears a voice telling him to "'Do things. . . . Keep the doors open.'" Suddenly, almost as an epiphany, the pastor realizes that rather than agree with the church members that the doors to the church should be locked to keep out the homeless and vandals, he must do something. Instead of viewing his profession, as he has done in the past, as a "*hiding place*" or "*sanctuary,*" he knows that he must take action. The words of his uncle about their "gifts" live in his memory: "To be chosen in such a way is, he said, both a blessing and a curse" (207). He decides not only to leave the church doors open but also to "leave blankets in the vestibule. He will leave food, water, books, soap, towels, toothbrushes, clean clothes. He will leave toys, puzzles." The final image is of the pastor diving "to the bottom of the baptismal—*immersion*," a fitting word for the new direction he has decided to take.

NOTES

Chapter One: Introduction

1. S. Keith Graham, "Southern Foibles Eloquently Washed Ashore," *Atlanta Journal and Constitution Book Review,* 30 Sept. 1990, 1.

2. Jill McCorkle, interview, 6 June 1998.

3. Jill McCorkle, "What to Wear on the First Day at Lumberton High . . . ," an essay written for Algonquin Books of Chapel Hill, 1990.

4. Jill McCorkle, *First Words: Earliest Writing From Favorite Contemporary Authors,* ed. Paul Mandelbaum (Chapel Hill, N.C.: Algonquin, 1993).

5. McCorkle, "What to Wear."

6. Lee Smith, interview, 24 Aug. 1998.

7. McCorkle, interview.

8. Jill McCorkle, letter to Bennett, Jan. 1994.

9. Jill McCorkle, Series Folder 154.2, ms. coll., University of North Carolina at Chapel Hill.

10. Lynn Z. Bloom, "Jill McCorkle," *Contemporary Fiction Writers of the South,* ed. Joseph M. Flora and Robert Bain (Westport, Conn.: Greenwood, 1993), p. 296.

11. McCorkle, "What to Wear."

12. Elinor Ann Walker, "Redefining Southern Fiction: Josephine Humphreys and Jill McCorkle" (Ph.D. dissertation, University of North Carolina at Chapel Hill, 1994), 12.

13. McCorkle, interview.

14. Alice McDermott, "Back Home To Carolina," *New York Times Book Review,* 11 Oct. 1987, 1.

15. Bloom, "McCorkle," 301.

Chapter Two: *The Cheer Leader*

1. Jill McCorkle, *The Cheer Leader* (Chapel Hill, N.C.: Algonquin, 1984). All parenthetical citations for *The Cheer Leader* are from this edition.

2. Annie Gottlieb, "Manic Jo and Romantic Sam," *New York Times Book Review,* 7 Oct. 1984, 9.

3. Walker, "Redefining Southern Fiction," 53.

Chapter Three: *July 7th*

1. Gottlieb, 9; Brian Ferguson-Avery, "Announcing the Birth of Another Southern Writer," *Americus (Ga.) Times Recorder,* 14 Nov. 1996.

2. Jill McCorkle, *July 7th* (Chapel Hill, N.C.: Algonquin, 1984): 90. All parenthetical citations for *July 7th* are from this edition.

Chapter Four: *Tending to Virginia*

1. Jill McCorkle, *Tending to Virginia* (Chapel Hill, N.C.: Algonquin, 1987). All parenthetical citations for *Tending to Virginia* are from this edition.

2. Diane Manuel, review of *Tending to Virginia, Christian Science Monitor* (Eastern edition) 5 Jan. 1988, 18; Jeris Cassel, review of *Tending to Virginia, Library Journal* (1 Nov. 1996): 200; Pearl K. Bell, review of *Tending to Virginia, New Republic,* 29 Feb. 1988, 40.

3. Stead, 26.

4. Linda Tate, *A Southern Weave of Women: Fiction of the Contemporary South* (Athens: University of Georgia Press, 1994), 27.

5. Ibid., 24.

6. Ibid., 33.

Chapter Five: *Ferris Beach*

1. McCorkle, interview.

2. Ron Loewinsohn, "The World Across the Street," *New York Times Book Review,* 7 Oct. 1990, 10; Graham, "Southern Foibles," 1; Laurie Muchnick, "Southern Discomfort," *Voice,* 20 Nov. 1990, 82; Elise Chase, review of *Ferris Beach, Library Journal* (15 Sept. 1990): 102.

3. Jill McCorkle, *Ferris Beach* (Chapel Hill, N.C.: Algonquin, 1990), 56. All parenthetical citations for *Ferris Beach* are from this edition.

4. Carol Pearson and Katherine Pope, *The Female Hero in American Literature* (New York: Bowker, 1981).

5. Joan Schultz, "Orphaning as Resistance," *The Female Tradition in Southern Literature: Essays on Southern Women Writers,* ed. Carol S. Manning (Champaign: University of Illinois Press, 1993), 92.

6. Pearson, and Pope, "The Female Hero," 121.

Chapter Six: *Crash Diet: Stories*

1. Jill McCorkle, *Crash Diet: Stories* (Chapel Hill, N.C.: Algonquin, 1992). All parenthetical citations for *Crash Diet: Stories* are from this edition.

2. Walker, "Redefining Southern Fiction," 11, 139.

3. Jill McCorkle, on-line interview, 1995. <http://206.103.79.6/voices/jillm.htm>.

4. Walker, "Redefining Southern Fiction," 11, 130.

5. Jack Butler, "Is There Anything Worse Than a Man," *New York Times Book Review,* 14 June 1992, 15; Greg Johnson, "Heart Troubles," *Georgia Review* 46 (1992): 363.

6. Butler, "Is There Anything Worse," 15–16.

7. A few examples of the woman/bird characterization can be found in Kate Chopin's *The Awakening,* Eudora Welty's *The Optimist's Daughter,* Susan Glaspell's *Trifles,* and Bobbie Ann Mason's "Shiloh."

8. Johnson, 363.

9. Butler, "Is There Anything Worse," 16.

10. Sandra M. Gilbert and Susan Gubar, *The Madwoman in the Attic: The Woman Writer and the Nineteenth-Century Literary Imagination* (New Haven, Conn.: Yale University Press, 1979), 42.

11. Butler, 16; Johnson, 363.

12. Walker, 127.

Chapter Seven: *Carolina Moon*

1. Henry L. Carrigan, Jr., review of *Carolina Moon, Library Journal* (1 Nov. 1996): 107.

2. Jill McCorkle, *Carolina Moon,* (Chapel Hill, N.C.: Algonquin, 1996). All parenthetical citations for *Carolina Moon* are from this edition.

3. "A Conversation with Jill McCorkle," Reader's Circle Web Site, <http://www.randomhouse.com/BB/readerscircle/mccorkle/guide_p.html>.

4. Bloom, "McCorkle," 300.

5. Gilbert and Gubar, *Madwoman,* 36.

Chapter Eight: *Final Vinyl Days and Other Stories*

1. Jill McCorkle, *Final Vinyl Days and Other Stories* (Chapel Hill, N.C.: Algonquin, 1998). All parenthetical citations for *Final Vinyl Days* are from this edition.

2. Review of *Final Vinyl Days, Publishers Weekly,* 20 April 1998, 44; *Kirkus Reviews,* 66 (1 April 1998): 427.

3. Donna Seaman, review of *Final Vinyl Days, Booklist* 94:17 (1 May 1998): 1502, 1504; Meg Wolitzer, "Hard Cases," *New York Times Book Review,* 19 July 1998, 23; Ann H. Fisher, review of *Final Vinyl Days, Library Journal* 123:7 (15 April 1998): 118.

4. McCorkle, interview.
5. Ibid.

BIBLIOGRAPHY

Books by McCorkle

Carolina Moon. Chapel Hill, N.C.: Algonquin, 1996.

Cheer Leader, The. Chapel Hill, N.C.: Algonquin, 1984.

Crash Diet: Stories. Chapel Hill, N.C.: Algonquin, 1992.

Ferris Beach. Chapel Hill, N.C.: Algonquin, 1990.

Final Vinyl Days and Other Stories. Chapel Hill, N.C.: Algonquin, 1998.

July 7th. Chapel Hill, N.C.: Algonquin, 1984.

Tending to Virginia. Chapel Hill, N.C.: Algonquin, 1987; London: Jonathan Cape, 1989.

Selected Essays by McCorkle

"Achievement, Tradition, Vision, 1842–1992." *Hollins Critic,* Oct. 1991, 54.

"Blacktop Carnival." *Southern Living* 25 (Oct. 1990), 172.

"Cathy, Now and Then." In *Between Friends,* ed. Mickey Pearlman (Boston: Houghton, 1994).

First Words: Earliest Writing From Favorite Contemporary Authors. Ed. Paul Mandelbaum. Chapel Hill, N.C.: Algonquin, 1993.

"Listening to Flannery." *The Flannery O'Connor Bulletin* 24 (1995–1996): 127–28.

"Our Summer Vacations." *Southern Living* 25 (Jan. 1990), 110–11.

"What to Wear on the First Day at Lumberton High." In *Algonkian,* newsletter published by Algonquin Books of Chapel Hill, 1990.

Secondary Bibliography

Books and Articles

Bennett, Barbara. *Comic Visions, Female Voices: Contemporary Women Novelists and Southern Humor.* Baton Rouge: Louisiana State University Press, 1998. A discussion of humor in the works of female southern novelists since 1970, including *Ferris Beach, Tending to Virginia, The Cheer Leader,* and *July 7th.*

————. "'Reality Burst Forth': Truth, Lies, and Secrets in the Novels of Jill McCorkle." *The Southern Quarterly: A Journal of the Arts in the South* 36.1 (Fall 1997): 107–22. Explores lies and self-delusion as an overriding theme in the five novels of McCorkle.

Bloom, Lynn Z. "Jill McCorkle." In *Contemporary Fiction Writers of the South,* ed. Joseph M. Flora and Robert Bain (Westport, Conn.: Greenwood, 1993): 295–302. A short overview of McCorkle's life and works up through *Ferris Beach.*

Summer, Bob. "Jill McCorkle." *Publishers Weekly* (12 Oct. 1990): 44–45. A short biographical and critical article discussing McCorkle's common topics and general themes, including a brief discussion of people and the popular culture that have influenced her work.

Tate, Linda. *A Southern Weave of Women: Fiction of the Contemporary South.* Athens: University of Georgia Press, 1994. Explores the role of women and families in the literature of the contemporary South. Chapter one focuses in part on *Tending to Virginia* and the intergenerational bonds that hold families together.

Walker, Elinor Ann. "Redefining Southern Fiction: Josephine Humphreys and Jill McCorkle." Ph.D. dissertation, University of North Carolina at Chapel Hill, 1994. Argues that McCorkle, along with Josephine Humphreys, creates strong female characters in an attempt to define space and to gain acceptance for a more self-assured female identity in the South.

BIBLIOGRAPHY

———. "Celebrating Voice and Life in Jill McCorkle's *Crash Diet*." *Notes on Contemporary Literature* 23.1 (1993): 11–12. Discusses several of the women characters in *Crash Diet* as they attempt to find their voices and re-create a new and stronger self.

Interviews

"A Conversation with Jill McCorkle." Reader's Circle Web Site, <http://www.randomhouse.com/BB/readerscircle/mccorkle/guide_p.html>.

Graeber, L. "Biding Time in the Secretarial Pool." *New York Times Book Review,* 14 June 1992, 16.

Harlan, Megan. "Talking With Jill McCorkle: A Southern Storyteller." *Newsday,* 29 Sept. 1996, C33.

"Jill McCorkle." 1995. <http://206.103.79.6/voices/jillm.htm>.

Jordon, Shirley Marie, ed. *Broken Silences: Interviews With Black and White Women Writers.* New Brunswick, N.J.: Rutgers University Press, 1993.

Lesser, Ellen. "Voices With Stories To Tell: A Conversation With Jill McCorkle." *Southern Review* 26 (1990): 53–64.

O'Leary, Janice. "Interview With Jill McCorkle." *Agni* 45 (1997): 194–200.

Selected Reviews

The Cheer Leader *and* July 7th

Chappell, Fred. "Powder Puffs & Loose Peanuts." *Chronicles of Culture* 9, no. 7 (July 1985): 6–7.

Gottlieb, Annie. "Manic Jo and Romantic Sam." *New York Times Book Review,* 7 Oct. 1984, 9.

BIBLIOGRAPHY

Hegi, Ursula. "A Couple of Novels from the Same Southern Milieu." *Los Angeles Times,* 15 Nov. 1984, section 5, p. 34.

Tending to Virginia
Hill, Jane. "Novel Links Three Generations of Southern Women." *Atlanta Journal & Constitution,* 13 Sept. 1987, 1.

McDermott, Alice. "Back Home To Carolina." *New York Times Book Review,* 11 Oct. 1987, 1.

Stead, Deborah. "Holding On and Moving On." *The New York Times Book Review* (11 Oct. 1987): 26.

Ferris Beach
Graham, S. Keith. "Southern Foibles Eloquently Washed Ashore." *Atlanta Journal & Constitution Book Review,* 30 Sept. 1990, 1.

Loewinsohn, Ron. "The World Across the Street." *New York Times Book Review,* 7 Oct. 1990, 10.

Muchnick, Laurie. "Southern Discomfort." *Voice,* 20 Nov. 1990.

Crash Diet: Stories
Butler, Jack. "Is There Anything Worse Than a Man." *New York Times Book Review,* 14 June 1992.

Johnson, Greg. "Author Thrives On 'Crash Diet.'" *Atlanta Journal & Constitution* (17 May 1992), section N, p. 8.

———. "Heart Troubles." *Georgia Review,* 46 (1992): 363.

Carolina Moon
Carey, Jacqueline. *New York Times Book Review,* 15 Dec. 1996, 12.

Holzer, Helen. *Atlanta Journal & Constitution,* 22 Sept. 1996, L09.

Samway, Patrick H. *America* 175 (21 Sept. 1996): 31.

BIBLIOGRAPHY

Final Vinyl Days and Other Stories

Broderick, Pat. "Feasting On the Fear of the Unknown." *San Diego Union-Tribune,* 7 June 1998.

Stepp, Holly. "Southern Stories Are Funny, Sad, Weird—and Good." *Lexington Herald-Leader,* 19 July 1998.

Wolitzer, Meg. "Hard Case." *New York Times Book Review,* 19 July 1998, 23.

INDEX